Efficiency in the Public Sector

Efficiency in the Public Sector

The Theory and Practice of Cost–Benefit Analysis

Edited by

Alan Williams
University of York, UK

and

Emilio Giardina
University of Catania, Italy

Edward Elgar

© Alan Williams, Emilio Giardina, 1993

All rights reserved. No part of this publication may be reproduced, stored in a retrieval system, or transmitted in any form or by any means, electronic, mechanical, photocopying, recording, or otherwise without the prior permission of the publisher.

Published by
Edward Elgar Publishing Limited
Gower House
Croft Road
Aldershot
Hants GU11 3HR
England

Edward Elgar Publishing Company
Old Post Road
Brookfield
Vermont 05036
USA

A CIP catalogue record for this book is available from the British Library

Library of Congress Cataloging-in-Publication Data
Efficiency in the public sector: the theory and practice of cost
 –benefit analysis/edited by Alan Williams and Emilio Giardina.
   192p. 23cm.
   Includes index.
   1. Expenditures, Public—Cost effectiveness. 2. Government spending policy.   I. Williams, Alan, 1927–   . II. Giardina, Emilio.
HJ7451.E34   1993
336.3'9—dc20   92–42192
                                                              CIP

ISBN 1 85278 812 7

Printed in Great Britain at the University Press, Cambridge

Contents

List of Figures and Tables	vii
List of Contributors	ix
Introduction	xi
Alan Williams and Emilio Giardina	

PART I GENERAL METHODOLOGY

1. Public and private sector project appraisal: a comparative evaluation   3
   David Mayston
2. Cost–benefit analysis and the theory of resource allocation   26
   Salvatore Enrico Battiato
3. Information precision and multicriteria evaluation methods   43
   G. Munda, P. Nijkamp and P. Rietveld
4. Cost–benefit analysis: applied welfare economics or general decision aid?   65
   Alan Williams

PART II PARTICULAR APPLICATIONS

5. Cost–benefit analysis of transport projects   83
   Chris Nash
6. Cost–benefit analysis in health and health care: fine in practice, but does is work in theory?   106
   Michael F. Drummond

PART III POLICY CONTEXT

7. Project finance and decentralization in public investment   129
   David Mayston and Gilberto Muraro
8. The role of analysts in the public investment decision-making process   146
   Giacomo Pignataro
9. The public decision-making process and cost–benefit analysis   158
   Ilde Rizzo

Index   171

Figures and Tables

FIGURES

1.1	The cost of changes in project specification	6
1.2	Multiple internal rates of return	12
1.3	Mutually exclusive projects	13
1.4	Net social benefit	15
3.1	The structure of an evaluation process	46
3.2	A systematic representation of a concerted planning evaluation methodology	47
3.3	Chain of transformations	52
6.1	Components of economic evaluation	110
6.2	Quality-adjusted life-years added by treatment	111
6.3	The relevant changes in a comparison of the economic efficiency of treatment	117

TABLES

1.1	The project cycle	5
3.1	Possible combinations of information measurement levels and uncertainty	50
3.2	A typology of multidimensional evaluation methods	53
3.3	Activity and decision profile of a compound decision problem	57
3.4	Confrontation of a requirement profile with a given planning problem	58
3.5	An impact matrix	58
5.1	Costs and benefits of a road scheme	84
5.2	Example of a stated preference question	86
5.3	Resource values of time per person	87
5.4	Average cost per casualty, by severity	88
5.5	Costs and benefits of road schemes: the Leitch framework	91
5.6	Brigg Inner Relief Road, impact groups	94
5.7	Birmingham–London/Basingstoke electrification	97

5.8	Comparison of net present values of two rail investment programmes	98
6.1	Comparative costs of two programmes for mental illness patients	109
6.2	'League table' of costs and QALYs for selected health care interventions	111
6.3	Valuation matrix for 70 respondents	119
6.4	Mean daily health state 'utilities' in the general population sample	120

Contributors

S.E. Battiato, University of Catania, Italy.
M.F. Drummond, University of York, England.
E. Giardina, University of Catania, Italy.
D. Mayston, University of York, England.
G. Munda, Institute for Systems Engineering and Informatics, Italy.
G. Muraro, University of Padua, Italy.
C.A. Nash, University of Leeds, England.
P. Nijkamp, Free University of Amsterdam, Netherlands.
G. Pignataro, University of Catania, Italy,
P. Rietveld, Free University of Amsterdam, Netherlands.
I. Rizzo, University of Reggio Calabria, Italy.
A. Williams, University of York, England.

Introduction

Alan Williams and Emilio Giardina

This book provides a critical overview of the role of cost–benefit analysis (CBA) in improving the efficiency of public sector investment appraisal by tracing the evolution of the scientific debate in this field. The theoretical and practical implications of such a debate are dealt with in an European perspective.

Particularly during the 1960s, economists had strongly advocated the use of cost–benefit analysis in this context, since by then it had been developed so as to be the preferred method, both from a theoretical and from a practical point of view. But growing attention has been paid in the subsequent literature to its shortcomings, mainly referring to its concentration on efficiency, and its consequent difficulty in dealing with the many other objectives which the public decision maker has to pursue. As a consequence of this debate, a wide range of viewpoints can be identified: most economists still consider CBA to be a normative tool of applied welfare economics, whilst others, though maintaining its principles, see its role as providing a useful information system aimed at correcting information asymmetries. The relevance of this latter role becomes more obvious when certain features of public decision making are taken into account, especially when the political bias of public decisions is considered to be relevant. The most extreme manifestation of this viewpoint rejects the use of CBA altogether and looks for alternative evaluation methods such as multicriteria techniques.

In this book the main streams of this debate are presented. The case studies cover one of the most traditional fields of application – transport – and a more recent and less conventional sector of application – health – to indicate how the flexibility of the analysis permits adaptation according to the features of the projects to be evaluated.

Part I rehearses the general theoretical framework on which the other chapters are based. Chapter 1 examines how public and private sector project evaluation techniques compare, and the lessons which can be drawn from this comparison for public sector project evaluation. The *discounted cash flow* criterion is presented as the private sector investment appraisal rule which best promotes the interest of shareholders. The extension of this rule to public sector investment appraisal requires the inclusion of consumer benefits alongside the financial return to the producer. Attention is also paid to the treatment of risk and uncertainty in both private and public sector appraisal and the role of the *ex post* monitoring of the returns of the investment is stressed. However the actual adoption of such techniques in the public sector is likely to depend on the introduction of suitable managerial incentives, which have often been lacking.

In Chapter 2 the peculiarities of public sector analysis with respect to private sector analysis are stressed. The chapter is devoted to the theoretical foundations of CBA in the context of Pareto criteria for an efficient resource allocation. It first considers objectives and constraints in public investment decision making, and discusses which effects can be ignored and which must be taken into consideration. It then examines some problems which arise in the evaluation of effects in monetary terms with regard to efficiency and equity. The chapter also considers some problems related to the choice of the social discount rate. All these problems are discussed bearing in mind a number of common criticisms of CBA.

In Chapter 3 the main shortcomings of such an approach are pointed out, especially as far as its one-dimensional orientation is concerned. Multicriteria evaluation techniques are presented as more appropriate analytical tools for analysing conflicting policy objectives. Moreover it is argued that, in order to deal with real-world problems, these methods must be able to handle the imprecision and uncertainty often present in the available information. One of the messages coming from the chapter is that it is not plausible to establish *a priori* which method it is better to use as a general rule, such choices being context-dependent; therefore the problem is to choose the right method for the particular problem. In this context a typological approach has been illustrated and some properties desirable for decision support systems for environmental problems have been indicated.

With the above considerations in mind, Chapter 4 addresses the general issue of the role that evaluation methodologies can play in the decision-making process. As far as CBA is concerned, it is argued that, if such a technique is to serve as a useful decision aid in a democratic society, those practising it must be prepared to cast off the Paretian 'straitjacket' where necessary, especially its alleged neglect of distribution (or equity) issues. CBA concerns, then, anything that people value (however they value it) and its purpose is to help ensure that the value of the additional things that are provided by some project is greater than the value of the things that have to be sacrificed. By becoming more versatile in this way, the conduct of CBA also becomes more risky, because it is operating in a minefield of political and quasi-political issues which need to be exposed and circumnavigated with great care.

Part II offers two particular applications of the use of evaluation techniques, contrasting the performance of CBA and multicriteria evaluation methods in the field of transport and in the field of health and health care.

Chapter 5 offers a critique of CBA as applied to transport projects. It first considers those items that are usually valued in money terms in a transport project appraisal and, then, in turn, a number of common criticisms of transport project appraisal. Following this, alternative approaches to appraisal, including objective-based and, multicriteria techniques, are considered. It is concluded that these alternative techniques do not overcome the problems raised with respect to CBA in the case of transport projects. Moreover, they are concerned with simplifying and making more consistent the final decision taking, rather than presenting information on the costs and benefits as perceived by those directly affected by the projects. As such, they are complementary to, rather than competitive with, CBA as a technique. The use of a disaggregated form of CBA, such as Community Impact Evaluation, which presents detailed information on all effects by incidence group, is recommended.

The aim of Chapter 6 is to give an assessment of the current state of CBA in health care. The special characteristics of health and health care are outlined since they partly condition the application of CBA in this field. Attention is also paid to the precise formulations of CBA used in the appraisal of alternatives in health and health care. The chapter also examines particular aspects of CBA in practice, including the selection of alternatives for appraisal, the assessment of costs and benefits and the analysis of distributive effects.

In Part III, project appraisal is examined in the light of the special features of the public decision-making process. Chapter 7 considers the special problems that arise in decentralized systems when there is likely to be conflict between the national government's desire to exercise control over public expenditure as a whole and the local government's desire to further the welfare of its own citizens. Intergovernmental financial arrangements need to be tailored so as to generate incentives for the efficient use of centrally provided funds, which in turn requires at least the capacity to monitor how such funds are being deployed., This often leads national governments to specify the kind of project appraisal they expect to have conducted before funds are made available, and possibly to earmark such funds to ensure that they achieve what the national governments intend. This conflict also arises between the European Commission and the national governments of the European Community, and for the same reasons.

Chapter 8 deals with the role of analysts in the public investment decision-making process. It argues that, since there is no 'objective' way of carrying out the economic evaluation of projects, its outcome mainly depends on the way analysts' work is influenced by their relationship with decision makers and other people involved in the decision-making process. These relationships are analysed within different institutional frameworks, characterized on the basis of the location of analysts within the decision-making process and the nature of the analysts' appointment (whether as bureaucrats or as external consultants). The way different methodologies (CBA and multicriteria methods) can constrain the evaluation actually carried out by analysts is considered. It is finally argued that, if analysts have to provide the general public with transparent information on different projects, external consultants are better motivated than others to do so, but the results of their work have to be made public.

The aim of Chapter 9 is to explore the relationship between CBA, the multicriteria approach and the public decision-making process. The main idea is that the characteristics of public decision making enable participants to circumvent the 'objectivity' of CBA. At the same time, the systematic application of evaluation techniques is considered to affect positively the functioning of the process itself, because the information base is improved. From this point of view, the impact of CBA and multicriteria techniques ,is found to depend on the features of the public decision-making process. If it is unbiased, the multicriteria approach can be considered as an improvement on CBA since the scope of evaluation is enlarged. If it is biased, however, the answer is less straightforward.

With growing pressure for harmonization within the European Community, there is bound to be growing pressure to standardize the evaluation techniques by which decisions are made relating to public investment, especially where EC financial support is requested. This has already led to tensions between the Commission and member states over whether the appropriate evaluative *processes* were undertaken. But what this volume shows is that formally requiring evaluation to be done will not guarantee that *effective* evaluation will be done, according to set methodological criteria. An appropriate incentive structure needs to be created, and greater openness about criteria and information ensured. It is a challenge to both analysts and decision makers to ensure that the European communal experience of public project evaluation in the next 30 years is not simply a rerun of our individual experiences over the past 30 years!

ACKNOWLEDGEMENTS

Much of the work which has gone into the creation of this volume was financed by Research Grants No. 8701155.10 and No. 8900763.10 from the Italian National Research Council.

PART I

General Methodology

1. Public and Private Sector Project Appraisal: A Comparative Evaluation*

David Mayston

1 INTRODUCTION

In this chapter we examine how public and private sector project evaluation techniques compare, and the lessons which can be drawn from this comparison for public sector project evaluation. Since individual public sector projects frequently involve the expenditure of large sums of public money, improving the process of project evaluation is an important step towards improving the management of public capital resources.

Whilst the process of privatization of public utilities has in recent years reduced the size of the directly owned public sector in some European Community (EC) countries, such as the UK, it has typically done so without substantially reducing the monopolistic nature of these industries. We will therefore include in our discussion an examination of the extent to which the above lessons apply also to these newly privatized public utilities. In addition we will stress the key roles of both the *ex ante* project evaluation of expected returns and their riskiness, and the *ex post* monitoring of the value for money obtained from investment in the project.

2 CAPITAL RESOURCE MANAGEMENT

The importance of sound project evaluation, in both the public and the private sectors, can be seen from the consequences of failing to carry out such evaluation adequately. These consequences are chiefly twofold:

a. a failure of the project to generate a positive return, measured according to an appropriate criterion, that is sufficient to make the project worth-

---

* This chapter draws upon research work carried out by the author under the ESRC-funded research project WB04250012 on Public Capital Expenditure, Resource Management and Capital Accounting.

while. Numerous examples of such project failure are to be found in both the public and the private sectors (see, for example, Henderson, 1977; Kharbanda and Stallworthy, 1983; Bignell and Fortune, 1984).

b. the accumulation of excess capacity and underutilized capital facilities, whenever the evaluation procedures for new investment, and the incentives for saving capital, are weak. There may then be a tendency, particularly in the public sector, towards favouring capital-using new-build solutions to service provision (see Mayston, 1990), rather than towards improving the management of existing capital assets.

The significance of sound project evaluation can also be seen by examining its role within the *project cycle* that embodies the stages required for successful *project management* in both public and private sectors, as in Table 1.1. We may also note here the contribution which different techniques of financial and economic analysis can make to each stage of the project cycle.

The individual supporting techniques available are discussed in greater detail in Bowman and Ash (1987), Brealey and Myers (1988), Cleland and King (1983), Flanagan and Norman (1983), French (1989), Heitger and Matulich (1986), and Wilson and McHugh (1987).

Figure 1.1 illustrates the rising costs of changing the specifications of the project after the initial conception and evaluation phases in which the project is still capital in 'putty' form, before setting as 'clay' as embodied capital (see Bliss, 1968; Cleland and King, 1983). A comparison of Table 1.1 and Figure 1.1 shows that the available techniques of economic analysis are applicable at just that time when it is relatively costless to change the project specifications. A failure to apply adequately these techniques, including those of risk analysis, in these initial stages of the investment project will then result either in costly later changes in the project specification (as in the case of the Nimrod project: House of Commons Defence Committee, 1987–8) or in inappropriate projects being adopted.

The failure of many public sector projects, such as Concorde and the Humber Bridge, to yield a positive economic return, despite their technical engineering success (albeit achieved often at high financial cost), can be seen to result largely from a failure to apply adequate economic and financial analysis at the initial conception and evaluation phases. Concorde was in essence wrong in conception. It involved extrapolating the existing aviation trends in the wrong direction, of faster travel at increasing cost for an exclusive clientele. In doing so, it exposed the investment to high risk because of (1) the high fuel usage per passenger mile and consequent sensitivity to fuel price increases, (2) the unknown development costs of the new technology required to be developed, and (3) its greater unreliability for potential passengers, owing to teething problems with the new technology,

Table 1.1   The project cycle

I.   *The Conception Phase*

Supporting techniques: analysis of economic, social, political and technological trends; identification of competitive advantage; corporate strategy planning.

II. *The Validation Phase*

Supporting techniques: demand forecasting; market research; risk analysis; life-cycle costing; decision analysis; *project evaluation*; net present value analysis; break-even analysis; sensitivity analysis; product testing.

III. *The Planning Phase*

Supporting techniques: critical path analysis; network analysis; programme evaluation and review technique (PERT); budgeting; standard costing; matrix management; contracting.

IV. *The Construction Phase*

Supporting techniques: cost/profit/responsibility centres; matrix management; variance analysis; bar charts/Gantt project progress charts; milestone reports.

V.   *The Operational Phase*

Supporting techniques: production and sales monitoring variance analysis; depreciation accounting; output quality testing; monitoring consumer response.

VI. *The Divestment Phase*

Supporting techniques: identification of optimal timing of divestment; *ex post* investment appraisal; identification of lessons to be learnt for future projects.

---

that undermined the advantages of greater maximum speed. In contrast, the vastly more successful (private sector) wide-bodied jets, such as the Boeing 747, involved an extrapolation of existing technology, in the direction of a

Figure 1.1 The cost of changes in project specification

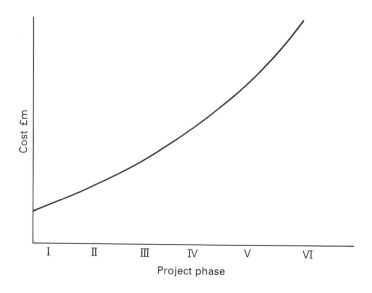

greater volume of aircraft at decreasing average cost per passenger mile, to a rapidly expanding mass market.

How relevant is it that Boeing was a private sector producer, whereas Concorde was a project sponsored by the British and French governments? Clearly projects that are wrong in conception are not unique to the public sector. Sinclair's C5 design for a low-cost battery-driven car in the UK proved a predictable financial disaster, given the lack of protection which its design offered to its occupant in city traffic conditions. The private sector Davy Corporation in the UK has in the past been driven to near financial collapse by its underestimation of the costs of a large engineering project in which it became involved.

However there are two main reasons why the risk of project failure on a substantial scale may in general be greater in the public sector than the private sector. The first is that the threat of bankruptcy and take-over may provide a greater brake upon such projects either being initiated or proceeding beyond their initial stages. The second involves a recognition of the strong *political* element in public sector decision making on the initiation and continuation of projects. Thus, in the cases of Concorde and the Humber Bridge, political patronage, national and regional prestige, Britain's entry into the EC, local employment considerations and their political impact,

Public and Private Sector Project Appraisal: A Comparative Evaluation 7

local government reorganization and other political factors have influenced the decisions to continue with these projects.

One important feature of political decision making is its relatively myopic nature, with considerations beyond the next election at times given relatively little weight, despite the long-lived nature of many investment projects. In contrast, much of the literature on private sector investment policy (for example, Ansoff, 1969; Bowman and Ash, 1987; Porter, 1985) stresses the need to consider investment decisions within a well-formulated long-term *strategic* framework. Similarly Porter (1990) emphasizes the importance of private sector investment taking a broad strategic view of where the comparative advantage of the nation lies, in order to secure synergy between the new investment and the existing industrial clusters of economic activity that are capable of exploiting this comparative advantage.

3 PRIVATE SECTOR INVESTMENT APPRAISAL

Against this background, let us now turn to a detailed examination of private sector investment appraisal criteria and their economic rationale, before next examining how relevant they are to the public sector. The strongest underlying economic rationale for a private sector investment criterion is that provided by Irving Fisher's Separation Theorem (Fisher, 1930; Hirshleifer, 1958) for the *net present value rule* (NPV).

The net present value of a project can be expressed as the discounted present value of the annual income, Y_t, generated by the project net of its initial investment cost I, over the T years of the life of the asset created by the investment; that is:

$$\text{NPV} = \frac{Y_1}{(1+r)} + \ldots + \frac{Y_t}{(1+r)^t} + \ldots + \frac{Y_T}{(1+r)^T} - I \quad (1.1)$$

where r is the prevailing rate of interest. Thus in the case of $r = 10$ per cent $= 0.10$, $Y_t = £12$m over each of the $T = 3$ years of the life of the project and an initial investment cost of $I = £15$m, this becomes in £m:

$$\text{NPV} = \frac{12}{(1.1)} + \frac{12}{(1.1)^2} + \frac{12}{(1.1)^3} - 15 = 14.84 \quad (1.1a)$$

The NPV calculation here takes into account the *time value of money*; that is, that income received later in the project is worth less, and hence discounted by a larger factor in (1.1), than the same amount of income received earlier. This reflects the fact that having to wait longer for income means a loss of additional interest that could have been obtained if it had been received earlier and invested in a bank earning interest in the intervening years.

The annual income at any time t is given by:

$$\text{INCOME} = \text{REVENUE} - \text{VARIABLE COSTS} \\ - \text{ADMIN.COSTS} - \text{TAX} \quad (1.2)$$

or in algebraic terms:

$$Y_t = R_t - TVC_t - TAC_t - X_t \quad (1.3)$$

That is, the income generated by the project at time t equals the gross revenue, R_t, from the sale of the output of the project, less the total variable cost, TVC_t, in producing the output, less the total administrative and distribution cost, TAC_t, and less the taxation, X_t, paid at time t. Y_t then represents the net operating *cash flow* that results from the project in period t. I in equation (1.1) represents the initial cash outflow on the capital investment in the project. The NPV formula (1.1) can also then be expressed as the *discounted cash flow* resulting from the project.

The net present value rule of investment appraisal is then:

$$\text{undertake the project if NPV} > 0 \\ \text{reject the project if NPV} \leq 0 \quad (1.4)$$

That is, undertake the project if its net present value is positive, and reject it if it is negative or zero.

We may next compare the above definition of the net annual income, Y_t, with the definition of annual *accounting profit*, P_t, after interest and taxation. We have annual profit to be given by:

$$\text{PROFIT} = \text{REVENUE} - \text{VARIABLE COSTS} \\ - \text{ADMINISTRATIVE COSTS} - \text{TAX} \\ - \text{DEPRECIATION} - \text{INTEREST} \quad (1.5)$$

or in algebraic terms:

$$P_t = R_t - TVC_t - TAC_t - X_t - D_t - N_t \quad (1.6)$$

involving the subtraction also of annual depreciation, D_t, and interest payments, N_t, from annual revenue. We assume here that turnover (that is, the revenue due from sales in period t) net of operating, distribution and administrative costs, is received, in cash in year t, with no net balance of debtors over trade creditors for each period.

From equations (1.3) and (1.6):

$$Y_t = P_t + D_t + N_t \qquad (1.7)$$

that is

$$\text{INCOME} = \text{PROFIT} + \text{DEPRECIATION} + \text{INTEREST} \qquad (1.8)$$

The net operating cash flow that is relevant to the computation of Y_t in equations (1.1) and (1.3) thus involves *adding back* the interest payments, N_t, at time t and the non-cash item of depreciation, D_t, at time t to accounting profit after interest and taxation. In other words, we cannot directly make use of accounting profit in the calculation of NPV in equation (1.1) and the investment criterion (1.4). Instead we must add back the two terms, of annual depreciation, D_t, and interest payments, N_t, to accounting profit, P_t, in equation (1.6) to obtain our desired measure Y_t of net operating cash flow, for use in equation (1.1) and the investment criterion (1.4).

4 ALTERNATIVE PRIVATE SECTOR INVESTMENT CRITERIA

We have so far identified the NPV investment appraisal rule (1.4) as the economically correct rule for private sector investment if the firm is to act in the best interests of its shareholders. Before we turn to an explicit consideration of how public sector investment criteria compare with this prescribed private sector investment criterion, we need first to note that the NPV approach is by no means the only private sector investment criterion in use in the private sector. Rather there are a number of other private sector investment criteria that we need to examine. These include: (1) *the accounting rate of return*, which we may define as

$$ARR_t = (P_t + N_t + X_t) / I \qquad (1.9)$$

$$= (R_t - TVC_t - TAC_t - D_t) / I \qquad (1.10)$$

$$= \text{PROFIT BEFORE INTEREST \& TAX} / \text{INVESTMENT OUTLAY} \qquad (1.11)$$

The investment decision rule is then to compare the accounting rate of return in each period with the prevailing before-tax rate of interest, and undertake the investment if the former is on average over the lifetime of the project greater than the latter.

However, if normal straight-line depreciation is used to calculate D_t, adequate allowance will not be made for the time value of money. The result of applying this decision rule is then potentially inconsistent with that of the discounted cash flow criterion, which we have identified above to be the correct investment criterion if the managers of a private sector firm are to act in the best interests of their shareholders. In addition, whilst the accounting rate of return measure (1.9) provides a measure of the gross *return on investment* (ROI), it does not take into account the precise amount of tax actually payable by the firm on the profits from the investment or the extent to which the shareholders of the firm are benefiting from financing part of the investment out of fixed interest debt.

(2) *the return on equity (ROE) criterion* in contrast looks at profits after tax, and after interest payments on the debt used in part to finance the investment. The return on equity then equals

$$ROE_t = [P_t / Q] = [P_t / (I - B)] \tag{1.12}$$

$$= \text{PROFIT AFTER INTEREST \& TAX} / \text{SHAREHOLDERS' FUNDS} \tag{1.13}$$

where Q is the amount of equity finance (as represented by the Shareholders' Funds in the firm's balance sheet) and B is the amount of debt used to finance the initial investment outlay I. The criterion is then that the investment should be undertaken if the ROE over the life of the project on average exceeds the prevailing rate of interest r. If conventional straight-line depreciation is used to compute P_t in equation (1.6), the ROE measure suffers from the same criticism of ignoring the time value of money cited above. If the interest rate on debt is constant over the life of the project, we may rewrite this criterion in terms of whether on average

$$[P_t + N_t] / I \quad \text{where } N_t = r.B \tag{1.14}$$

that is,

PROFIT LESS TAX PLUS INTEREST / INVESTMENT OUTLAY (1.15)

exceeds the prevailing rate of interest.

(3) *The pay-back period method*: that the total cash flows generated by the project within the first x years must exceed the initial capital outlay. The choice of x is here a number, such as five, determined in advance. This method in general suffers from the problems (a) that it ignores discounting, and therefore fails to take into account the time value of money, and (b) it ignores the size of cash flows after the first x years and hence has too short a time horizon. It appears to have developed in the private sector mainly as a crude adjustment for the uncertainty that may attach to profits after the end of the pay-back period.

However there is a special case where the pay-back period is consistent with the correct discounted cash flow approach. This occurs when the expected cash flows after the initial capital outlay are constant into the infinite future. We then have from equation (1.1) for the case of T tending to infinity that:

$$\text{NPV} = \frac{Y_1}{(r/100)} - I \qquad (1.16)$$

with the corresponding investment criterion being to undertake the investment if and only if:

$$\frac{Y_1}{(r/100)} > I \qquad (1.17)$$

Under the same assumption of constant annual cash flows from period one onwards, the pay-back criterion is

$$x.Y_1 > I \qquad (1.18)$$

For the choice of $x = (100/r)$, (1.18) is, however, perfectly consistent with the discounted cash flow criterion (1.17). Thus, if the prevailing interest rate, r, is 20 per cent, then the choice of $x = 5$ in the pay-back criterion is equivalent here to the application of the discounted cash flow criterion.

(4) *The internal rate of return (IRR) criterion*, which requires us to find that value, u, of the discount rate, s, that will equate the net discounted cash flow

$$ND = \frac{Y_1}{(1+s/100)} + \ldots + \frac{Y_t}{(1+s/100)^t} + \ldots + \frac{Y_t}{(1+s/100)^T} - I \qquad (1.19)$$

to zero. If the internal rate of return, s, exceeds the prevailing rate of interest, r, the criterion requires that the project be undertaken, but not otherwise.

However the IRR method itself suffers from the disadvantage that it is possible that there may exist more than one value to s. Thus, in Figure 1.2, *ND* equals zero at two values of the internal rate of return, 5 and 10 per cent. If the lower rate of 5 per cent is used in the assessment, and the prevailing rate of interest is 8 per cent, the project will be rejected. However at 8 per cent, the project in Figure 1.2 has a positive net discounted cash flow, *ND*, and therefore should be accepted under the discounted cash flow criterion. There is then a conflict between the recommendations of the IRR method and those of the NPV method.

It can be shown that so long as the cash flows, after the initial capital outlay, are all positive, the above problem of the internal rate of return taking on potentially more than one value will not occur. The ND curve will then slope downwards for all values of the discount rate, s, in equation (1.19). There will then be only one value to the internal rate of return: that value of the discount rate, s, at which *ND* is zero.

Figure 1.2 Multiple internal rates of return

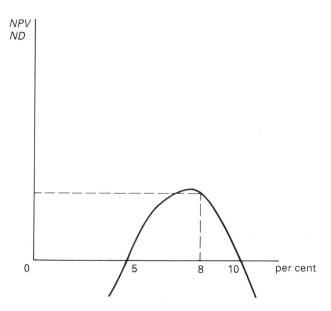

However, even here a problem arises in the case of *mutually exclusive projects*, such as two different development schemes for a given shopping centre. We will label these two mutually exclusive projects as projects I and II, with corresponding curves ND_I and ND_{II} in Figure 1.3. If we use the internal rate of return as the basis for selecting which of the two mutually exclusive projects to undertake, project II in Figure 1.3 has the larger internal rate of return. However at the prevailing rate of interest, r, in Figure 1.3, project II has a lower net discounted cash flow, ND_{II}, than project I. Again the two decision rules are in conflict. The internal rate of return criterion favours project II, but the theoretically correct net discounted cash flow criterion favours project I. Unless we know which is the theoretically correct decision rule, we may clearly make the wrong choice.

Figure 1.3   Mutually exclusive projects

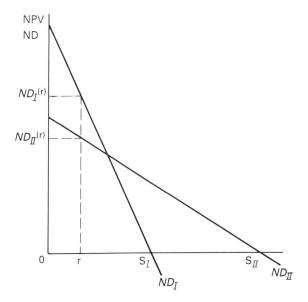

Again there is a special case where the above problem does not occur, that where the annual cash flows after the initial capital outlay are growing at the same constant growth rate over time for all the projects being compared, and this initial capital outlay is the same for all the projects. There will then be a single internal rate of return for each project, which will also provide a reliable indicator of which project has the highest net discounted cash flow, even for mutually exclusive projects. However, once the initial capital outlays or growth rates of the annual cash flows differ across the projects, the consistency of the two criteria is again no longer guaranteed.

5   COMPARISON WITH A PUBLIC SECTOR APPROACH

We have seen in the previous sections that a discounted present value of the cash flows generated by a project is the investment decision rule which will ensure that the managers of a private sector firm will act in the interests of its shareholders. However we have also seen that there are a number of investment decision rules that are used in the private sector that are typically in conflict with the present value approach and may therefore fail to look after the interests of the shareholders of the firm adequately.

In the public sector we clearly wish to avoid the pitfalls associated with these less than satisfactory private sector investment criteria, and attempt to ensure that the rule we choose is consistent with the present value approach. In this section we therefore compare the investment appraisal criteria used in the public sector to the discounted cash flow approach recommended for the private sector.

The first main difference is that the profit to the producing firm is generally an inadequate measure of the net benefit to society of the output of the firm. Rather than look just at the profit accruing to the owners of the firm, we need to take into account the fact that consumers will also typically benefit from the goods and services produced by the firm. In general the price which consumers pay to the producing firm understates the benefit which consumers derive from successive units of the output of the firm. One traditional measure of the benefit which consumers derive from the successive units of output is the price they are *willing to pay* for these units. The excess of the price consumers are willing to pay over the price they do actually pay, that is their 'consumer surplus' given by the area DJZ in Figure 1.4, is a traditional measure of the net benefit they derive from consuming the commodity in question (Marshall, 1920).

The total consumers' surplus may then be added to the producers' surplus, or operating profit, to yield the 'total net social benefit, NB_t, in period t. The producers' surplus is given by the area ZJH in Figure 1.4, being the excess of the market price p over the marginal cost of producing successive units of the output, less any fixed cost F_t involved in period t.

The question then arises as to how far we can translate our earlier analysis for private sector investment decisions to the public sector using the above measure of social benefit. There are a number of circumstances when we can make this translation directly:

a. when each individual in the society has a constant share in the total net social benefit NB_t, and is therefore in a parallel position to a shareholder in a private sector firm;

Figure 1.4 Net social benefit

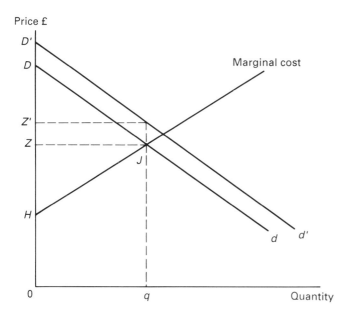

b. where society's preferences, as expressed through its elected government or other means, involve indifference between different ways of distributing a given social sum across different individuals in the society;
c. when there exist lump-sum transfers to optimize the distribution of income across individuals following the implementation of the project.

If they are to be consistent with a well-behaved transitive set of social preferences for all possible price changes, (a) and (b) can be shown to require that the strong restriction that each individual's income elasticities of demand are unity (see Silberberg, 1972; Mayston, 1993). In such a case we can make use of our earlier measure of consumers' surplus in our measure of social benefit ND_t in place of profit.

In order to avoid the strong assumption that all income elasticities of demand are unity, we can, however, more generally replace individual consumers' surpluses with the notion of 'Generalized Consumer Surplus', GCS^i, introduced in Mayston (1974). To avoid the restrictive assumption (c), and the notion of distributional indifference implicit in condition (b), we can make use of a weighted version of individual (generalized) consumers' surpluses, so that our measure of net social benefit now becomes:

$$NB_t = \sum_i w^i . GCS_t^i + c_t . (ZJH_t - F_t) \qquad (1.20)$$

where the subscript t denotes the fact that the size of these surpluses may vary over time. If all income elasticities of demand are unity, we may set $GCS^i = DJZ^i$ where DJZ^i is the area under individual i's demand curve. Further discussion of distributional considerations in cost–benefit analysis is contained in Salvatore Battiato's contribution to this volume.

We can also preserve our earlier notions of the time value of money by substituting NB_t in place of Y_t in equation (1.1) above in our calculation of the net present value of the investment project. *We have then generalized our earlier private sector investment criterion to a social cost–benefit investment criterion by taking into account not only the financial return to the producer but also the gain to the consumers of the project's output.*

In the case of a nationalized industry, the weight c_t on the producers' surplus in equation (1.20) can be set to achieve any desired feasible net revenue target, such as a break-even target or a 'required rate of return' (cf. Cmnd 7131, 1978). The principle of 'constrained maximization' is then equivalent here to increasing the weight c_t on the producers' surplus until this net revenue target is achieved. In general, however, individual consumer surpluses remain positive in equation (1.20), and hence need to be taken into account in a social project evaluation. Only if the demand curve (*Dd*) in Figure 1.4 is horizontal, as under a 'perfectly elastic' demand curve, will the consumers' surplus area *DJZ* become zero. Such a perfectly elastic demand curve will arise when the individual firm is operating in a perfectly competitive market. It is then a small part of the total market and the market price can be taken as a fair reflection of the value which consumers place upon another unit of its output. The excess of its revenue over its operating costs, as under the discounted cash flow investment criterion, can then be taken as a fair reflection of the social net benefit of the firm's output in period t. Under these conditions, a *private investment appraisal and a social cost–benefit appraisal of the firm increasing the output of its product are then equivalent*, so long as there are no additional factors to be taken into account. The list of such additional factors includes the possibility of 'externalities', such as pollution, from the firm's output, and the use by the firm of labour that would otherwise be unemployed. Both these factors imply that the market price of the relevant output or input may not reflect adequately its social opportunity cost.

Thus there are a number of special conditions, such as perfect competition without externalities, under which private sector and public sector investment criteria become equivalent. More generally, however, private sector investment criteria cannot be applied directly to the public sector in an unadjusted way. Instead we can take the most satisfactory private sector investment criterion identified above, that of the NPV rule and modify it by inserting the net social benefit measure (1.20), in place of simply the income, Y_t, to the producer, in the NPV formula (1.1) in order to obtain a satisfactory public sector investment criterion.

6 MANAGERIAL INCENTIVES

For many public sector activities, such as the supply of health, education and transport, the public sector producer represents a large part of the total market output. The demand curve for its output is then typically not perfectly elastic. The total consumers' surplus from its output is then typically positive rather than zero. To ignore any measure of the benefits to consumers in the investment criteria of public sector producers, as an earlier UK governmental White Paper on nationalized industries (Cmnd 7131, 1978) would implicitly have had us do, would be to regard the public sector simply as a revenue generator for the public exchequer.

If it is to serve a wider social role, and consumers are a key part of that society, then social cost–benefit analysis implies that we adopt the measure NB_t as our measure of net benefits to society in period t, rather than simply producers' profit. However the question then arises as to how we can provide incentives to the managers of public sector enterprises to achieve this wider objective. A similar problem arises in the context of the regulation of newly privatized natural monopolies, such as the electricity and water industries. A solution to this problem is provided by the notion of 'non-profit performance indicators' discussed in Maystone (1985). Under the simplifying assumption of distributional indifference, we may replace the weighted consumers' surplus term in equation (1.20) with

$$G_t = B_t(p_t) + \sum_j v_{jt} \cdot Q_{jt} \qquad (1.21)$$

where B_t is an index of the vector, p_t, of prices charged by the enterprise at time t evaluated at a reference standard of quality of service, Q_{jt} is an indicator of the quality of service in direction j (such as the quality of drinking water) provided by the enterprise and v_{jt} is an economic valuation on unit changes in this quality. Greater quality of service shifts the consumers' demand curve in Figure 1.4 to a higher level D'd' to an extent that is greater the larger is this economic valuation by consumers on such quality improvements.

There are, then, a number of ways of incorporating such performance indicators into the incentive framework for managers:

a. performance-related pay, such that the salary of the manager is an increasing function of both the profit of the enterprise in (1.20) and the benefit to consumers in (1.21), as dependent upon the prices charged by the enterprise and the quality of service delivered;
b. specification in the terms of the licence or contract for the enterprise continuing to be the supplier of quality of service targets;
c. financial penalties on the enterprise, such as through lower permitted price increases, for failing to achieve quality of service targets.

These possibilities, drawing on the experience of both the public and the private sectors, are discussed in more detail in Mayston (1985, 1986). By the use of the above incentive devices, which have been widely applied in the private sector, one would expect to be able to produce favourable behavioural consequences for managers in the public sector, encouraging them to take investment and production decisions in line with the wider social interest, including the interests of consumers.

7 RISK AND UNCERTAINTY

In private sector investment appraisal, the most easily applicable means of adjusting for risk and uncertainty that still has a strong theoretical justification is by use of a *risk adjusted discount factor* derived from the *capital asset pricing model* (Brealey and Myers, 1988). This has the effect in our discounted present value formula (1.1) of replacing the risk-free rate of interest, r, by the following risk-adjusted discount factor:

$$f = r + [E(r_m) - r].b \qquad (1.22)$$

$E(r_m)$ is here the expected return on the 'market portfolio' represented by movements in the Stock Exchange index of share prices and dividends on the shares represented in the index. The coefficient b is the 'beta coefficient' for the firm's investment, reflecting how far its returns are likely to be correlated with movements in the economy-wide Stock Exchange index.

The adjustment of the net present value criterion for private sector investment appraisal to accommodate considerations, of risk is then achieved by replacing r with f in equation (1.1), and replacing each period's income Y_t with the *expected value*, $E(Y_t)$, of income in period t. Again the income that is relevant here for private sector investment appraisal is net operating cash flow.

The type of risk that is reflected in the beta coefficient in equation (1.22) is that of *systematic risk*. This is the risk which remains even when shareholders in the private sector firm are fully diversified in their individual portfolios of shares. Such diversification can enable them to escape from the *specific risks* involved in investing in individual firms, such as the risk of the Managing Director suffering a heart attack. Such risks can be reduced asymptotically towards zero by spreading the individual shareholder's portfolio across a large number of individual shares. Because individual shareholders can easily diversify across a large number of firms in different parts of the economy, there is no need for each individual firm to worry in its investment appraisal about these specific risks (except in so far as they raise the possibility of costly bankruptcy for the firm).

However even after shareholders have diversified their holding of shares across the whole economy, there remain risks which cannot be diversified out of. These arise from the underlying 'systematic' uncertainty about how the whole economy will perform in the coming years. At any given future date, it is at present uncertain what the state of the international and national economy will be like, whether boom or recession of different possible levels. For the shareholder to invest in any particular firm will expose the shareholder in varying degrees to this underlying economy-wide uncertainty, according to which particular firms the shareholder invests in. If it is a firm in the steel industry, then the returns to investing in this industry are likely to be highly sensitive to changes in the general state of economic activity. Boom conditions are likely to mean a high demand for products, such as refrigerators, cars and machine tools, that use steel, and associated high capacity utilization and profits for the steel industry. The converse is likely to be true in times of recession. If the firm is a supermarket chain, then its profits are likely to be less sensitive to general economic conditions, with some countercyclical tendency for consumers to spend more on food, drink and household goods in times of recession when they cancel their foreign holidays and orders for new cars. To invest in supermarket shares then exposes the individual investor less to the risks of economy-wide fluctuations in economic activity than investing in the steel industry. There is then a correspondingly lower beta coefficient of the amount of systematic risk involved in investments in the supermarket trade in equation (1.22) than there would be for investments in the steel industry.

When we turn to investment in the public sector, it can be seen that the position of the taxpayer is rather similar to that of a diversified investor in the private sector, whenever the public sector itself holds a wide portfolio of investments. Arrow and Lind (1970) have argued that such a diversified portfolio for the public sector itself implies that no adjustment should be made for risk in public sector investment criteria. However this argument neglects the fact that diversification only removes specific risks. Systematic risks remain even after diversification. Moreover many of the types of investment traditionally made by the public sector are in industries that are quite sensitive to the general state of economic activity. These include the electricity, steel, shipbuilding and aircraft industries, where these are in public ownership. The extent of the systematic risk can be shown to increase with the extent of the ratio of fixed to variable cost involved in supplying the output. In many industries that are or have recently been in the public sector the ratio of fixed to variable costs is indeed high, tending to make them high-risk industries even when we focus only on systematic risk. Capital-intensive producers, such as steel and electricity, will then produce high returns when the economy is booming and their capacity is fully utilized, but substantially lower returns when the economy is in recession and they face excess capacity with high overhead costs that they cannot easily remove.

In other parts of the traditional public sector, such as investment in health and water, the sensitivity of demand to general economic activity may be much lower. In coal, transport and telecommunications there will be cases where the level of benefits is sensitive to the general state of economic activity and other cases where it is relatively insensitive. The general notion of systematic risk is therefore very relevant to the public sector. However, in contrast to the private sector where the random walk assumptions of the efficient capital market hypothesis may apply, one cannot necessarily assume in the public sector that uncertainty is multiplicative over time. One cannot then necessarily simply substitute the risk-adjusted discount factor of equation (1.22) in place of the risk-free interest rate r in equation (1.1), in the way private sector investment criteria (see Brealey and Myers, 1988) would suggest. Rather it may be necessary to make use of systematic risk in determining *certainty equivalents* of an uncertain stream of social benefits, before then discounting these multiplicatively at the risk-free rate in equation (1.1).

In some cost–benefit studies, there will be risks that fall not just on the general taxpayer, but on the individual consumer as well. One such case would be where there is a risk of a new road increasing the number of accidents, both fatal and non-fatal. In the case of non-fatal accidents, it may be possible to compensate the road-user through a public or private insurance scheme. The risks are then effectively diversified and systematic risks are again what matters. However in the case of fatal accidents, it is clearly more difficult to compensate the victims *ex post*, causing them to bear some element of specific risk *ex ante*. Additional adjustments then need to be made in the cost–benefit analysis for these forms of specific risks. The issues raised by attempting to value different states of health following intervention by the surgeon, or car accident, are discussed in greater length later in this volume.

When there are both systematic and specific risks, use may be made of the notion of the *expected utility* of different levels of social benefit, with private sector managerial tools such as decision trees (see French, 1989) then applicable also to the public sector to implement such notions. In addition the use of *sensitivity analysis*, aided by the use of computer spreadsheets, and *Monte Carlo simulations* that map out the consequences of potential changes in the underlying projected demand and costs of the project (see Brealey and Myers, 1988), can assist the project analyst in both the public and the private sectors in assessing the importance of uncertainty to the investment decision.

8   *EX POST* MONITORING

A final area that is in principle of some importance in the private sector is that of the *ex post* monitoring of the results of the investment. As we have noted in equation (1.6) above, profit in the private sector includes a subtraction for depreciation of the capital investment used to generate the income of the firm. The spreading out of the capital investment over the periods of time benefiting from its use that this involves represents highlighting in the company's accounts the fact that such capital investment has been incurred to generate the firm's income.

If the method of depreciation used is that of *annuity depreciation* (see Mayston, 1990), together with an adjustment for inflation in the asset values over time, it can be shown that a positive level of accounting profit throughout the life of the capital assets created by the investment project implies that a positive net present value has indeed been achieved *ex post* by the project. Depreciation in the accounts of the company would then represent the means by which the question of whether or not *value for money* is being achieved from the initial investment could be monitored. Unfortunately in practice the private sector rarely uses annuity depreciation. Rather it typically makes use of straight-line depreciation which fails to take into account the time value of money, as would be required for consistency with the present value approach. In addition, the private sector in the UK, apart from former nationalized industries such as gas and, water, rarely uses inflation accounting to adjust asset values (other than those of land and buildings), following the demise of the inflation accounting standard SSAP16 (ICAEW, 1989).

The result is that the depreciation figure in the accounts is typically understated, as a result of being based upon the outdated historic cost of the firm's assets, which itself understates their current value. The return on equity investment figure given by equation (1.12) is thus overstated owing to an overstated numerator and an understated denominator in the ratio on the right hand side of equation (1.12). An apparently satisfactory return on investment may then disguise a very low actual return on investment that is associated with a negative net present value to the investment in the company's assets.

Nevertheless the concept of *stewardship* and *value for money assessment* that in principle at least underlies private sector company accounting is still of relevance to the public sector, even though in practice the private sector often falls short of this ideal. Highlighting in the accounts of public authorities an appropriate indication of the capital input into the provision of public services, alongside the cost of other inputs, such as labour, would assist in the *ex post* monitoring of the extent to which annual benefit obtained from these services compares with the total cost of their provison, including capital costs. Use of annuity depreciation would then provide a method of depreciation consistent with the net present value approach.

Part of this annual assessment of benefits might be from performance indicators on the quality of service delivered, weighted by economic valuations, as in Mayston (1985), or through measures, such as Quality Adjusted Life Years (see Williams, 1985) for health services. If the annual benefit obtained does exceed the annual cost, inclusive of the annuity depreciation charge, then the net present value of the original investment will *ex post* be positive, thereby confirming that value for money has indeed been obtained from the original investment.

Largely because of the cash-based nature of its public expenditure funding, the non-trading public sector has until recently failed to adopt any such form of depreciation in its annual revenue accounts or any adequate form of capital accounting for fixed assets in its balance sheets. A partial exception to this has been the use by local authorities in the UK of debt charges based upon the outstanding debt of the authority. Where there is a high percentage of debt financing of the capital assets, the debt charges do, in some degree at least, highlight in the revenue accounts of the authority an indication of the annual capital cost of the original investment. Where poor value for money has been obtained from the original investment, a net deficit will result, as indeed is the case in the UK with the Humber Bridge whose accumulated financial deficit now stands at some £400m following low usage and low toll revenue (see Bignell and Fortune, 1984). Even the inclusion of consumer surplus estimates of the benefit of this low usage are unlikely to reverse this financial monument to the lack of value for money obtained from the original investment.

Such a capital charge also provides a further *managerial incentive* to ensure that value for money is obtained, on the principle that those making bad investment decisions should bear the cost of their mistakes. However the enforcement of this principle is itself made difficult by the relatively short periods of office of the politicians making the original investment and the long time span over which the asset needs to be monitored to ensure that value for money is obtained.

For local authorities that are only partly financed out of debt, or whose capital assets were acquired largely before the high inflation rates of the mid-1970s–1980s, the debt charge in the local authorities' revenue accounts and the use of the historic outstanding debt to represent the value of assets in the balance sheet will not provide sufficiently accurate capital cost data to monitor adequately the achievement of value for money. New proposals for capital accounting in local authorities have been recently proposed in the UK (CIPFA, 1989), though these have yet to be implemented. Similarly proposals for systematic capital charging have been introduced recently into the National Health Service (NHS), though a greater alignment of the incentives provided by the charging system with the needs of improved capital resource management is still required (Mayston, 1990).

9 CONCLUSION

We have seen that the private sector investment appraisal rule which promotes the interests of the shareholders is that of the discounted cash flow criterion discussed above. This can be extended to take into account risk and uncertainty by replacing the risk-free interest rate with the risk-adjusted discount factor, as given by equation (1.22) above. Several other investment decision rules in use in the private sector were found to fall short of the advantages of the discounted cash flow criterion, particularly through their neglect of the time value of money.

The discounted cash flow criterion in the private sector can be extended to an appropriate investment criterion in the public sector by including consumer benefits, alongside the financial return to the producer, in the discounted present value calculation. The treatment of risk in public sector investments is often superficial, and would benefit from inclusion of systematic risk considerations in determining certainty equivalents for use in the discounted present value analysis. Whilst this would be in line with best private sector practice, we may also note that the private sector itself has often failed to adopt best practice techniques, relying instead on cruder adjustments for uncertainty, such as the pay-back criterion.

It should be noted that several private sector investment criteria, such as those involving the accounting rate of return and the return on equity, were developed primarily as *ex post* performance measures for the achievements of the investment. Whilst the private sector often falls short of its own ideals, the public sector would gain from greater attention to the *ex post* monitoring of the returns on investment that are actually achieved. Finally there is scope for the application of managerial incentives in order to align more closely private and social behaviour. Without such changes in incentives, prescriptions and achievements may continue to diverge.

BIBLIOGRAPHY

Ansoff, H.I. (ed.) (1969), *Business Strategy*, Harmondsworth: Penguin.
Arrow, K. and Lind, R. (1970), 'Uncertainty and the Evaluation of Public Investment Decisions', *American Economic Review*, **60**, pp. 368–74.
Bignell, V. and Fortune, J. (1984), *Understanding Systems Failures*, Manchester: Manchester University Press.
Bliss, C.J. (1968), 'On Putty-Clay', *Review of Economic Studies,* **35**, pp. 105–32.
Bowman, C. and Ash, D. (1987), *Strategic Management*, London: Macmillan.
Brealey, R. and Myers, S. (1988), *Principles of Corporate Finance*, 3rd edn, London: McGraw-Hill.
Chartered Institute of Public Finance and Accountancy (1989), *Capital Accounting in Local Authorities: The Way Forward*, London: CIPFA.
Cleland, D.I. and King, W.R. (1983), *Systems Analysis and Project Management*, 3rd edn, London: McGraw-Hill.
Cmnd 7131 (1978), *The Nationalised Industries*, London: HMSO.
Copeland, T. and Weston, J. (1988), *Financial Theory and Corporate Policy*, 3rd edn, New York: Addison Wesley.
Fisher, I. (1930), *Theory of Interest*, London: Macmillan.
Flanagan, R. and Norman, G. (1983), *Life Cycle Costing for Construction*, London: RICS.
French, S. (1989), *Readings in Decision Analysis*, London: Chapman and Hall.
Heitger, L.E. and Matulich S. (1986), *Managerial Accounting*, 2nd edn, New York: McGraw-Hill.
Henderson, P.D. (1977), 'Two British Errors: Their Probable Size and Some Possible Lessons', *Oxford Economic Papers*, **29**, pp. 161–205.
Hirshleifer, J. (1958), 'On the Theory of Optimal Investment Decision', *Journal of Political Economy*, **66**, pp. 329–372.
House of Commons Defence Committee (1987–8), *The Procurement of Major Defence Equipment*, HC431, London: HMSO.
Institute of Chartered Accountants of England and Wales (1989), *Accounting Standards*, London: ICAEW.
Kharbanda, O.P. and Stallworthy, E.A. (1983), *How to Learn From Project Disasters*, London: Gower,.
Marshall, A. (1920), *Principles of Economics*, 8th edn, London: Macmillan.
Mayston, D.J. (1974), *The Idea of Social Choice*, London: Macmillan.
Mayston, D.J. (1985), 'Non-Profit Performance Indicators in the Public Sector', *Financial Accountability and Management*, **1**, pp. 51–74.
Mayston, D.J. (1986), 'Performance Indicators: Are They Performing?', D.J. Mayston and F. Terry (eds), *Public Domain 1986*, London: Public Finance Foundation, London.
Mayston, D.J. (1988), 'Solutions to the Capital Accounting Conundrum', *Public Finance and Accountancy*, October, pp. 13–15.

Mayston, D.J. (1989a), 'Capital Asset Accounting in Local Authorities', in *Accountability and Management in Public Sector Accounting*, London: Chartered Institute of Public Finance and Accountancy, pp. 113–40.

Mayston, D.J. (1989b), 'Public Sector Financial Management and Capital Asset Management', in *Accountability and Management in Public Sector Accounting*, London: Chartered Institute of Public Finance and Accountancy, pp. 92–106

Mayston, D.J. (1990), 'Managing Capital Resources in the NHS', in A. Culyer, A. Maynard and J. Posnett (eds), *Competition in Health Care*, London: Macmillan, pp. 138–77.

Mayston, D.J. (1993), 'Public Choice, Stability and Social Rationality', in W. Gerrard (ed.), *The Economics of Rationality*, London: Routledge, pp. 123–48.

Porter, M. (1985), *Competitive Advantage*, New York: Free Press.

Porter, M., (1990), *The Competitive Advantage of Nations*, London: Macmillan.

Silberberg, E. (1972), 'Duality and the Many Consumer's Surpluses', *American Economic Review*, **72**, pp. 942–952.

Williams, A. (1985), 'Economics of Coronary Bypass Grafting', *British Medical Journal*, (291), pp. 326–329.

Wilson, R. and McHugh, G. (1987), *Financial Analysis – a Managerial Introduction*, London: Cassell.

2. Cost–Benefit Analysis and the Theory of Resource Allocation

Salvatore Enrico Battiato

1 COST–BENEFIT ANALYSIS IN THE PUBLIC SECTOR: OBJECTIVES AND CONSTRAINTS IN PUBLIC INVESTMENT DECISION MAKING

Every rational economic agent faces the problem of seeking solutions which enable him to maximize his net benefits. To this purpose, in order to determine whether or not it is advantageous to adopt a particular choice, he tries to define and to quantify its possible effects. Since this concept of rationality should not be alien to any organized community, it is not possible to object in principle to the utilization of explicit criteria, and specific procedures to be followed, for the evaluation of public activities. What differentiates private analysis (financial appraisal) from public analysis (economic or social appraisal, or what we call cost–benefit analysis) is that the latter, as we shall see, adopts a social perspective.

In this perspective cost–benefit analysis (CBA) is the tool of *applied welfare economics* which connects the decision to perform an action with its effects, in terms of benefits and costs to all the members of a community. It therefore derives its rationale from the concept of 'Pareto improvement'. We will therefore dedicate this chapter to the theoretical foundations of CBA in the context of 'Pareto criteria' for an efficient resource allocation.

In CBA the decision maker has as his fundamental objective an increase in social welfare, which therefore constitutes the 'social profit' to be maximized. There is a general conviction that one of the basic objectives of governments is the improvement of the standard of living of the members of the community, and that an important gauge of this is the aggregate level of consumption per capita (UNIDO, 1972, pp. 29 ff). On the basis of this conviction, in CBA it is assumed that the amount of national income, or of national consumption, constitutes an adequate index of social welfare. Although it represents an important element, however, it is not the only one constituting social welfare. It is possible to identify other factors, such as the level of employment, the satisfaction of needs considered 'merit goods', the measure of national economic independence, the rate of economic growth, a reduction in inequality and so on. The consideration of these other elements raises the problem of determining the trade-off between them.

Since the problem is difficult to solve, CBA usually evaluates the projects exclusively in terms of maximization of the amount of goods and services available, subjecting the pursuit of this objective to the constraint of the satisfaction, to a certain fixed degree, of the other requirements mentioned. It is necessary to note, nevertheless, that, even in an evaluation of public investments limited to the aspects of efficiency alone, several problems may occur which cannot be ignored. For instance, it may be that the variations in the economic welfare of the community, even if they show a positive global net result, assume positive values for some people and negative values for others. In this case, there would still be an improvement in the efficiency of the system, but it would be extremely difficult to identify and evaluate the distributional effects one by one. To avoid these difficulties the *compensation principle* is usually adopted. According to this principle, if the present value of a project is positive, it should be undertaken regardless of who gains and loses. This is because, as long as the present value is positive, the gainers could compensate the losers and still have some net benefit left over.

In CBA methodologies the comparison between the situation with the project and the situation *without the project* can constitute a check that the compensation test is satisfied. The comparison method makes it possible to see the flow of net benefits (that is of benefits after costs) as the difference between the net benefits in the situation *with*, and the net benefits in the situation *without*. A positive net present benefit implies that, in any case, the gain is greater than the loss.

In the traditional CBA theory it is considered that, in the light of the compensation test, the projects with the highest net benefits, since they permit a potential compensation between the gainers and the losers (under this test, of course, the compensation is not actually paid), leave the community on a higher level of welfare compared to the situation without the project or compared to the situation with projects chosen according to other criteria. While ensuring in this way that we reach some position on the welfare frontier, we may use taxation and income supplementation as policy instruments to pay sufficient compensation to the losers.

It may be objected that one cannot say whether it is desirable that compensation be paid or not, in the absence of specific value judgements about the distribution of income. So the compensation test does not avoid the difficulties involved in evaluating with a Pareto criterion public investments which imply a redistribution of the income. But we shall return to this point later (see section 3).

2 IDENTIFICATION AND ESTIMATE OF THE RELEVANT EFFECTS OF INVESTMENT PROJECTS: MARKET PRICES, SHADOW PRICES AND ECONOMIC EFFICIENCY

Having established that the object of CBA is to evaluate investment projects in terms of maximization of the *net economic* benefit to the community, regardless of who will be the gainers and who the losers, it is possible to determine which effects can be ignored and which must be taken into consideration, and how the latter must be estimated (Muraro, 1988). With respect to the above object, in fact, we must consider relevant for the evaluation of the project all effects which imply a positive variation (benefit) or a negative variation (cost) in the consumption possibilities of the community. Therefore in CBA an effect which is external to the project-operating entity may be socially relevant.

According to widespread opinion, the external effects are relevant if they alter the production possibilities of firms or the satisfaction which consumers may draw from such a resource (technological external effects). In fact these effects constitute a real cost or a real benefit to the community. A similar consideration could be made with regard to the so-called indirect ('stemming from' or 'induced by') benefits (Nuti, 1987, pp. 52–4). The indirect benefits must be taken into account and added to the direct ones only if it is possible to demonstrate (1) that there are unutilized resources in the economy and (2) that the project is able to stimulate a demand which otherwise would not be expressed . In fact, if there is full employment, it is not possible to expand certain activities, except at the cost of the contraction of others, and indirect benefits find compensation in the market. In this case the indirect benefits, as in the case of monetary external effects, refer to the distribution of the income, not to its amount .

Costs and benefits may be summed and compared only after they have been reduced to a common yardstick. As we know, the usual technique is to value the quantity of each commodity by the price which the users are willing to pay for it. Since there is no market in the public sector, CBA may be seen as the extension to this sector of an efficient price system. The basic hypothesis is that social welfare cannot be conceived of as something different from the welfare of each single member of the community. Therefore, in the absence of market prices or when the market fails. it is necessary to seek solutions which can guarantee that the results of the CBA will be as close as possible to the preferences of the members of the community.

In CBA, when market prices do not reflect the social value of the outputs and inputs considered because of failure in market functioning, it is necessary to have recourse to 'shadow' prices. This definition underlines the fact that such prices do not exist in reality; they are account prices able to represent the 'true' social cost and the 'true' social benefit of some effects of the project. In the light of the above requirements, the derivation of shadow prices is made according to the principle of the 'sovereignty of the consumer' and the consumer's willingness to pay constitutes the principal yardstick for reference.

Public investment projects often also count among their effects benefits and costs for which no price exists. These effects relate to goods such as human life, time, environment and so on, goods which are not subject to any direct market estimate. To take them into consideration, the analyst must attribute to them a monetary value. In these cases also shadow prices are resorted to; the criteria for fixing these are similar to those followed in the preceding case. In particular the advantages are measured on the basis of how much those who benefit are prepared to pay for them. Similarly the costs are represented by the amount those who bear the disadvantages are prepared to accept as compensation for bearing them willingly.[1] Finally there are effects, usually defined as 'incommensurables', of which it is possible to make only an analytical list.

The derivation techniques of shadow prices are controversial from both a theoretical and a practical point of view;[2] nevertheless they are based on economic criteria and the analyst must demonstrate the economic validity of the choice made. It is generally considered that adjustments made by means of shadow prices increase the possibilities of making an efficient decision, compared both to cases in which distorted market prices are used and to those in which important effects of the project are left out of the evaluation.

From the above brief indications the difficulties and problems implicated in recourse to shadow prices emerge clearly. Therefore, when the imperfections are not too great, it is preferable to use market prices. Even if the latter, as a result of a defect in the functioning of the market itself, do not reflect individual preferences exactly, they are nevertheless in some way correlated to them. Therefore it is necessary to use caution in the placement or modification of these by means of postulated or derived prices, constructed by means of exercises whose real validity cannot always be checked (on this point see Mishan, 1988).

In the evaluation of investment projects, even where the use of shadow prices is limited, there is still a certain margin of discretion for analysts; there are also many aspects which imply a 'political choice' (the fixing of the pay-back period and the social rate of time preference, the evaluation of externalities and so on). This margin of discretion exists also in the company accounting system of the private sector, even if it is limited by the existence of conventions and regulations which are universally recognized and accepted.

In the same way certain time-hallowed conventions and officially established practice rules limit the margin of discretion of CBA.

In operational experience this type of problem may be solved through an official system of national parameters and through the preparation of official manuals and 'instructions' containing a guide to CBA techniques with examples of its application, information regarding the political hypotheses on which it is based, technical parameters and so on.

3 COST–BENEFIT ANALYSIS AND DISTRIBUTIONAL ASPECTS

As we have seen, the economic welfare of a community may be represented in a satisfactory way by the total amount of its national income or consumption; the general aim of public investment is therefore the maximization of this value.

National income and consumption have three dimensions: the first regards quantity, the second distribution, the third modes of distribution. The aspects characterizing the first dimension are concerned with efficiency. The other two dimensions are more concerned with the concept of equity. In CBA only the first dimension is usually considered, so that the concept of efficiency is separated from that of equity. Therefore the role of CBA as an instrument for improving allocative efficiency is based on the hypothesis that distribution objectives and allocation objectives can be kept distinct.

This does not imply that the objective function of the decision-making entity cannot include other possible variables. In particular, the emphasis placed on the necessity to operate efficiently in resource allocation does not imply that the community, by means of its political representatives, is indifferent to the distribution of investment effects in time and space. For the implementation of redistribution strategies, taxes and subsidies are considered suitable instruments, both to reach the redistribution objective in general and to correct possible effects of the investment considered unfavourable from the point of view of a fair distribution of income.

Only in extreme cases, in which these instruments may not be used or in which substantial political reasons make it impossible to distinguish aspects of efficiency from those of equity, is it acceptable to insert distributional considerations into CBA. In these cases the conflict existing between efficiency and equity is usually solved by evaluating the projects in terms of maximization of the national income and imposing on this objective the obligation to satisfy distribution requirements to a given measure. By adopting this method it is possible to impose a limit by allotting, for example, a percentage of the resources to be invested to specific geographic areas.

Some authors do not share this view, because it does not take political objectives into account; these may be important, even if they are considered irrelevant or not measurable under a strictly economic profile. For example, it has been observed that one reason for political decision makers showing little enthusiasm for CBA lies in the fact that in the traditional approach this concentrates only on aspects of allocative efficiency. Those responsible for political decisions, in fact, attribute great importance to the many and various social aspects of collective decision making, aspects which may be noted and which must be considered in the political process (on this point see Pearce and Nash, 1981).

With reference to the social aspects of collective decision making, it is believed that the multiple objectives of organized communities in the last analysis reduce to the two fundamental and interdependent objectives of increasing available resources (development objective) and improving their interpersonal distribution (equity objective). On the basis of the stated interdependence of the two objectives a number of attempts have been made, especially on the theoretical level, to include considerations of distribution in CBA.

The topics covered in this part of the economics literature include situations in which, as well as the usual 'first best' constraints due to technology and scarcity of resources, there are other constraints present in the system. In such situations, given the existing constraints (institutional, political, legislative and so on), it is unlikely that a public intervention will be able to solve the problems connected with distribution by means of efficient transfers of resources and taxation, and therefore in these cases the objectives of efficiency and equity are interdependent and consequently inseparable (see Stiglitz, 1988; Petretto, 1987). In this case it is believed that the choice of suitable public investments itself may constitute an alternative instrument with which to reach redistribution objectives.

In order to determine the contribution of the project to social welfare, it is therefore necessary to measure the net benefit, taking into account also the effects in terms of distribution. Apart from the specific characteristics of each different contribution, in general also in this approach the dimension of the individual net benefits depends on willingness to pay and this, in its turn, depends on individual income.

It may be disputed, however, that market prices express the effective utility accruing to or withdrawn from the various social groups. With the unfair distribution which is characteristic of the real world, only if the marginal utility of the income were constant would the evaluation at market prices of the effects of the project reflect the preferences of individuals. In fact the identification of the social welfare function with that of a single representative individual is correct only if we assume that individual preferences have a common unitary structure compared to income.[3] But this assumption is not realistic and there are no objective reasons why it should be generally accepted.

In the opposite case, it is necessary to consider the utility of each single individual and therefore to measure benefits and costs with some coefficient which is able to express the utility accruing to or withdrawn from people. Thus the desirability of the project depends on the way in which the gains and losses of the different subjects involved are 'weighed' (see Appendix 1).

As we have seen, willingness to pay depends on the incomes of individuals. This means that the monetary values of the effects of the project must be modified with a factor related to the incomes of the individuals who bear its costs and/or enjoy its benefits.

In the traditional approach, these values are weighed with the factor 1. This weighting factor is appropriate if the present distribution of income is considered acceptable,[4] so that one monetary unit's worth of benefit is of benefit is of equivalent social value regardless of the subject to whom it accrues (see Williams, 1990). As a consequence, the evaluation of benefits and costs on the basis of hypotheses of income distribution different from that which favours the existing scenario requires the utilization of a weighting factor different from 1.

In research concerned with problems specific to developing countries, it is furthermore underlined that, even considering only the development objective, there is still the problem of establishing how much the single units of income generated by the project contribute to the realization of this objective. Only assuming that marginally all the units contribute in equal measure to development is it correct to evaluate them all in the same manner.

In the opposite case, it is important, for example, to establish how the costs and benefits of the project are distributed among individuals and among geographic areas, and whether the units of income produced by the project increase consumption or investment. Therefore, if the objective of the community is a given rate of development for which a given level of investment is necessary, until this level is reached a higher value must be attributed to the units of income destined for investment. In fact, if the general instruments of economic policy do not make it possible to reach the desired level of investment, because of the presence of constraints of any type, other instruments must be used, among them the choice of projects (Squire and Van Der Tak, 1975; Brent, 1990).

Although presented technically in different ways, the methodologies examined here are characterized above all by the use of a system of 'weights' with which, in substance, the results of the traditional cost–benefit analysis of a project may be modified. It is substantially an extension of the criterion of shadow prices, with the difference, however, that the shadow price, in these cases, is established on the basis not only of economic criteria but also of social criteria concerning equity. This shadow price serves to determine the weight to be attributed to the consumption of each subject (see Appendix 2).

Such a value may not be determined objectively,[5] since it implies an underlying value judgement. Because of this, the system of 'weights' must be built in such a way as to include values related to real characteristics of the economy, such as the existing distribution of income, the degree of economic development. Since these evaluations are of a largely political nature, as they reflect the conflicts and tensions present in society, it is necessary to have recourse to the political authority in order to establish the 'weights' with which to ponder benefits and costs accruing to the various subjects. Following this line, in passing from theory to practice, it becomes essential to depend on a political authority which decides in advance on a suitable national system of 'weights', given the objectives pursued (UNIDO, 1972).

To express different objectives the custom has been to define first of all certain 'efficiency shadow prices' traditionally derived from a simulation of the functioning of a perfect competitive market. With these it is possible to measure the effects of the project on the amount of goods and services available. At the second stage, other shadow prices, such as those just described, are used to express the contribution of the project to the realization of other national objectives and are called 'social shadow prices'.

Given the different objectives, the two types of shadow price are not mutually exclusive. Squire and Van Der Tak (1975), for example, recommend the evaluation of the effects of projects by means of market prices or efficiency shadow prices, and successively (and separately) the weighting of these values with social shadow prices. The same authors underline the difficulties connected with the adoption of social shadow prices and recommend the use of these in the evaluation of those projects for which there is reason to believe that their utilization could modify the final decision.

Moreover, by keeping the objectives of allocative efficiency distinct from those of equity, it is possible to establish how much a project contributes to the increase in social welfare, in terms both of an increase in the flow of goods and services available and of a redistribution of income (Harberger, 1983). Only in this way is it possible to determine the cost, in terms of efficiency, of the redistribution movement and, as a consequence of this, to define the instruments for its implementation which will reduce loss of welfare to a minimum.

In the most recent experiences of some supranational institutions, and in particular of the World Bank, efficiency shadow prices are normally used while social shadow prices are still being experimented with. Social shadow prices are applied by means of adjusting the results obtained with market prices and with efficiency shadow prices. In this way the decision maker may immediately grasp the difference between the results obtained from traditional analysis and those of the analysis carried out according to the methods described above.[6]

Another approach to incorporating distributional consideration in CBA is to ascertain the effects of public investments on the existing income distribution. To assess this impact some alternative indicators are commonly employed: Lorenz Curves, Gini Coefficient, the poverty index.

4 THE SOCIAL DISCOUNT RATE

The effects of many investments are realized over a long period of time. In order to compare the costs and benefits it is necessary to render them homogeneous, given the widespread conviction that one monetary unit available today is worth more than one monetary unit available tomorrow. Therefore the costs to be borne, and the benefits to be realized, in the future must be discounted in order to determine their present value. As we know, the factor which expresses a market evaluation regarding the availability of resources over time, in terms of both 'time preference' and 'productivity of capital', is the rate of interest, which represents the price of 'money'.

In the private sector each company, in the discounting operation, refers to the market interest rate which is relevant in its case; for instance, the discount factor private companies use is $1/1+r$, where r is the rate of interest which the company must pay for the money it borrows. (see Mayston, above). If the market were to work as in the model of perfect competition we should have only one interest rate and this, reflecting the opportunity cost of the resources, would be the efficient price of 'money' at various moments in time.

In reality the capital market does not work in a satisfactory manner but produces a variety of interest rates. Because of this, a problem arises as to which of the different market rates should be used by the public sector. It is necessary to choose, for example, either the rate at which the government can contract debts or the rate applied to the median taxpayer, or to establish an average rate. In any case, whatever the rate chosen, its amount will probably be influenced by taxes and subsidies in such a way as to distort it.

It is easy to see how, also for the interest rate, the problem of the inefficiency of market prices and of their replacement by shadow prices arises once again. Economics literature on this subject is rich in contributions, defining the theoretical principles and establishing the criteria for deriving an efficient discount rate which could be adopted in the various situations present in the public sector (see Mishan, 1988, pp. 286 ff).

Even in a perfect market, the rate of interest would not be the optimal discount rate. Therefore, also in this case, it may not be appropriate to use the market interest rate as a discount rate. If the individuals who benefit from the project are the same as those who pay the costs, we can simply use their marginal rate of substitution, how willing they are to trade off the reduction in current consumption for gains in future consumption. As we have seen above, the rate at which consumers are willing to substitute consumption today for consumption in the future (their time preference) would equal the rate at which it is technically possible to substitute consumption today for consumption in the future (the opportunity cost rate). In a perfect market, these common rates are also equal to the market rate of interest. In the public sector the market rate of interest would therefore be used as the discount rate.

But in the case of most long-lived projects, those who benefit from a project are often not those who paid its costs: subsequent generations receive the benefits. Individuals might ignore the effects of investment on members of future generations who were not their heirs. Therefore the social time preference rate could differ from individual time preference rates.

The choice of a discount rate is fundamental in any evaluation of long-term projects; a project which looks advantageous if a rate of 5 per cent is adopted may prove disadvantageous at a rate of 12 per cent. In the case described above, and in other similar cases,[7] the main problem is the relationship between the society's marginal rate of substitution of one generation's income for another's on the one hand, and the market rate of interest on the other. Economists are not always in agreement on the social time preference, the extent to which the government would use policy instruments to achieve the appropriate intergenerational distribution of income and, as a result, the way to evaluate increments of income of different generations.

For these reasons, as an alternative to the approach which tends to determine the shadow price of resources over time according to purely economic criteria, it is possible to underline the political aspects connected with the choice of a suitable discount rate for the public sector. With the problem noted above, the view is favoured that the choice of discount rate should be left to decision makers. Of course this form of delegation does not exactly meet the Paretian requirements for a change in welfare.

In the experience of several countries, Italy included, the shadow price in question, the so-called *social discount rate*, constitutes a 'national parameter' which is fixed directly by the political authorities.

5 COST–BENEFIT ANALYSIS AND NATIONAL PLANNING

CBA plays an important part above all in the processes of planning, because project analysis and planning are two closely linked activities. In CBA of public investment projects, while some of the variables considered regard the specific project under examination, others may be established only on a national level. CBA, therefore, may not be carried out in a satisfactory manner outside any context of planning.[8]

With reference to the Italian application, for instance, in the preliminary planning phase, the macroeconomic objectives and strategies are defined, the sectors and/or territorial areas in which to operate are located, the parameters of evaluation and the choice criteria fixed, the financial resources available determined. Later the programme will be articulated in annual operational plans containing specific investment projects, feasible and workable according to a rigid schedule. Each project must be consistent with the objectives of the programme, and its contribution to the achievement of the established objectives must be quantifiable. In this planning model, the preparation and evaluation of an operational plan of investment is a complex business, requiring the acquisition and analysis of a considerable mass of data, of an institutional, technical and economic nature. Planning, therefore, must clearly be the result of decisions produced by several institutions, and the outcome of a variety of specializations.

Planning through decentralized choices is the result of a process in which the central planning authority interacts with the other central and sub-central organisms involved in the programme. In the organizational and administrative context described, the interests of various institutional agents are rendered comparable by the decision-making process. This mechanism sees CBA as a series of rules and instructions which are binding for both the analysts responsible for evaluation and those involved in checking the same.

In conclusion, the model described above simulates a market mechanism featuring competition among public spending centres, an efficient price system through CBA, and a 'visible hand' through the planning process. If the planning process is carried out correctly it is possible to build a concrete and realistic operational plan in which the projects giving the highest yield are selected. Some authors do not share this view, because the current evaluation practice ignores interactions between the proposed projects. In the experience of many countries, each spending centre evaluates its own project independently, and the current evaluation process offers little opportunity for routine evaluation of the overall investment policy.

Some researchers indicate that there are errors due to the failure to consider pairwise interactions. If this is so, conventional procedures may result in systematic bias. If the bias is towards overstatement, wasteful investments may be misidentified as potentially beneficial. Those who share this point of view also define an alternative approach shifting the evaluation emphasis from projects to programmes (see Hoehn and Randall, 1989, and the bibliography therein).

6 COST–BENEFIT ANALYSIS AND PUBLIC CHOICE

In spite of theoretical and operational efforts to enforce the rule of allocative efficiency, public investment projects in many countries do not always conform to the criteria of profitability. So the maximization of social welfare is a recognized objective, accepted in words but not concretely pursued.

Recently, in an attempt to explain the reluctance of decision makers to accept the rule of allocative efficiency, research has been carried out in the direction of an analysis of the behaviour of those involved in the formulation and implementation of collective decisions on public investments (see Battiato, 1990; Giardina, 1990). Part III of this book is devoted to this aspect of the problem.

'Rationalization' in public activities constitutes a social need today more than in the past, however. The political–institutional articulation and the many different fields of intervention of the public sector, the complex nature of the programmes and, above all, the size of the financial resources controlled by this sector (now around 50 per cent of GNP in many industrialized countries) greatly increase the risk of inconsistencies between the various actions and of wastage of the available resources. It therefore becomes necessary to elaborate and adopt techniques to decide, to implement and to monitor the public actions on the basis of efficiency criteria. Of all these techniques, CBA is the one which best puts into practice the allocative efficiency rule.[9]

CBA may be seen as an information system relevant for allocative efficiency; obviously the purpose of CBA is to aid collective decision making, not to determine it. The data it supplies can be combined with other data provided by other systems; the CBA information system is important, therefore, even if it is not decisive. There have been many criticisms concerning the limits of CBA (see Schmid, 1989; Florio, 1990); nevertheless its use has become commonplace over the last few decades, as an official instrument of evaluation of investment projects.

Like any other intellectual discipline used in the pursuit of allocative efficiency, in carrying out public activities, it limits the freedom of individuals as well as the discretion of decision makers. Since decision makers are ostensibly obliged to pursue the objective of allocative efficiency, the preferences dictated by their personal interests as decision makers should be irrelevant. CBA must therefore be evaluated not for the degree of acceptance it enjoys from these individuals, but for its relevance to the social objective of allocative efficiency. The use of CBA, however, is not sufficient alone to bring about a radical alteration in the behaviour of decision makers. Such a change in behaviour may be obtained only if other reforms of the process of formulating and executing collective decisions are introduced besides CBA.

CBA also has the advantage of reducing the unequal distribution of information existing between citizens, politicians and bureaucrats, with reference to allocative efficiency. The existence of different levels of information is a reality to be found also inside decision making entities, and attributes an advantage to those who are 'better informed'. These, thanks to the information available to them, are able to pilot the final choice in the direction they desire.

CBA may contribute to a reduction of information asymmetry by supplying a data base common to all those involved in the decision-making process. In the absence of such an instrument, information is likely to become the object of an exchange which is distorted by a variety of circumstances (Battiato, 1988). CBA is not able to eliminate the presence of particular interests, but it can reduce the effect of these. CBA supplies and distributes information regarding the allocative efficiency of investment choices. In this way it increases the possibility for citizens to discover inefficient behaviour in the politicians responsible for collective decision making; it also allows politicians to reveal and prevent inefficient behaviour on the part of top-level bureaucrats, and these better to control their subordinates' actions.

NOTES

1. Methodologies and techniques for attributing a monetary value to these goods are discussed in Part II of this book. On the possible differences between 'willingness to pay' and 'willingness to accept' as a general problem, see Hanemann (1991).
2. On shadow prices in general see Drèze and Stern (1987) and the bibliography therein; see also Schofield (1989), pp. 53 ff; Hammond, (1988); Petretto (1987).
3. Therefore the proportion in which commodities are bought (that is the composition of the individual 'consumption basket') does not vary with a variation in income.
4. On this point, some authors, noting that the evaluations on which CBA is based favour the status quo, underline the conservative nature of this (see Campen, 1986).
5. With regard to the various attempts to measure this value in order to convert the measure of the benefits and costs at market prices in terms of variation in the utility of those interested see Brent (1990), pp. 56 ff.
6. For a critical analysis of the experience of the World Bank, see Leff (1985).
7. For instance, according to the 'isolation paradox', there are two rates of time preference: one when the investor acts 'in isolation', and one when he acts 'socially' with others (on this point see Pearce and Nash, 1981, pp. 144–5).

8. Bearing in mind this interdependence, CBA may still supply operators with useful information even in cases where no plan or programme exists.
9. Since it is not possible to deal with other techniques here, we will mention in passing only *multicriteria analysis*, to which Chapter 3 of this book is devoted.

BIBLIOGRAPHY

Battiato, S.E. (1988), 'Modelli di Analisi Benefici–Costi, processo di formazione delle scelte collettive e miglioramento dei risultati dell'azione pubblica', in *Annali della Facoltà di Economia e commercio dell' Università di Catania*, Vol. xxxiii, pp. 3–70.

Battiato, S.E. (1990), 'Analisi Benefici-Costi e sistema politico', *Nuovi Isas Papers*, (3), pp. 43–81.

Brent, R.J. (1990), *Projects Appraisal for Developing Countries*, New York: Harvester Wheatsheaf.

Campen, J.T. (1986), *Benefit, Cost and Beyond. The Political Economy of Benefit–Cost Analysis*, Cambridge, Mass.: Bollinger Publishing Company.

Drèze, J. and Stern, N., 1987, 'The Theory of Cost–Benefit Analysis', in A.J. Auerbach and M. Feldstein (eds), *Handbook of Public Economics*, *II*, Amsterdam: North-Holland pp. 909–89.

Florio M. (1990), 'Cost–Benefit Analysis and the Control of Public Expenditure: An Assessment of British Experience in the 1980s', *Journal of Public Policy*, **10**, (2), pp. 103–31.

Giardina, E. (1990), 'L'Analisi Costi–Benefici e il processo decisionale pubblico', paper presented to the meeting, *La valutazione economica dei progetti pubblici: un approccio settori di intervento*, 8 June, FORMEZ, Naples.

Hammond P. (1988), 'Principles for Evaluating Public Projects', in P.G. Hare (ed.), *Surveys in Public Sector Economics*, New York: Basil Blackwell, pp. 15–44.

Hanemann W.M. (1991), 'Willingness to Pay and Willingness to Accept: How Much Can They Differ?', *American Economic Review*, June, pp. 635–47.

Harberger, A.C. (1983), 'Basic Needs versus Distributional Weights in Social Cost–Benefit Analysis', in R. H. Haveman and J. Margolis (eds), *Public Expenditure and Policy Analysis*, 3rd edn, Boston, Mass.: Houghton Mifflin Co., pp. 105–26.

Hoehn, J.P. and Randall, A. (1989), 'Too Many Proposals Pass the Benefit Cost Test', *American Economic Review*, June, pp. 544–51.

Leff, N.H. (1985), 'The Use of Policy-Science Tools in Public-Sector Decision Making: Social Benefit–Cost Analysis in the World Bank', *Kyklos*, I, pp. 60–76.

Mishan, E.J. (1988), *Cost–Benefit Analysis*, 4th edn, London: George Allen & Unwin.

Muraro, G. (1988), 'Il problema degli obiettivi nella valutazione degli investimenti pubblici', in *Economia Pubblica*, (1–2), pp. 3–10.

Nuti, F. (1987), *L'analisi costi–benefici*, Bologna: Il Mulino.

Pearce, D.W. and Nash, C.A. (1981), *The Social Appraisal of Projects*, New York: J. Wiley and Sons.

Petretto, A. (1987), 'La valutazione dei costi e dei benefici dei progetti di investimento pubblico: premesse teoriche', *Lezioni di Analisi Costi–Benefici*, Naples: FORMEZ, pp. 17–90.

Schmid, A.A. (1989), *Benefit–Cost Analysis: A Political Economy Approach*, Boulder, Col.: Westview Press.

Schofield, J.A. (1989), *Cost–Benefit Analysis in Urban & Regional Planning*, revised paperback edition, London: Unwin Hyman.

Squire, L. and Van Der Tak, H.G. (1975), *Economic Analysis of Projects*, Baltimore, Md.: Johns Hopkins University Press.

Stiglitz, J.E. (1988), *Economics of the Public Sector*, 2nd edn, New York: Norton.

United Nations Industrial Development Organization (UNIDO) (1972), *Guidelines for Project Evaluation*, New York: United Nations Publication.

Williams, A. (1990), 'Some Methodological Issues in the Use of Cost–Benefit Analysis', in *Annali della Facoltà di Economia e Commercio dell' Università di Catania*, Vol. XXXV.

APPENDIX 1

We assume that a given community of H individuals has a function of individualistic welfare of the type

$$W = W[U_1(S_1), \ldots, U_h(S_h), \ldots, U_H(S_H)], \quad \text{(A1)}$$

in which S_h is the aggregate consumption of the individual h; differentiating, we obtain

$$dW = \sum_{h=1}^{H} \beta_h dS_h, \quad \text{(A2)}$$

with

$$\beta_h = \frac{\delta W}{\delta U_h} \frac{\delta U_h}{\delta S_h}. \quad \text{(A2a)}$$

Indicating with $dW_h = \beta_h dS_h$ the variation of the welfare of the individual h, β_h measures the marginal utility of h for a variation in its consumption dS.

Assuming $\beta_h = \beta$, that is the same for all the individuals, if $dW_h > 0$ for each individual, of necessity we shall have $dW > 0$, and if $\beta > 0$, then

$$\sum_{h=1}^{H} dS_h > 0. \quad \text{(A3)}$$

If β is not the same for all the individuals, it is necessary to consider the division of the net benefit among them, or at least among the social group. Indicating the latter with the index g ($g = 1, \ldots, G$), we may write

$$NB_g = \beta_g \Delta S_g = \Delta W_g, \quad \text{(A4)}$$

so that

$$NB = \sum_{g=1}^{G} \beta_g NB_g. \quad \text{(A5)}$$

Only if β_g is suitably determined for every g may the net benefit estimated with CBA come close to the real one, and that is

$$NB = dW.$$

APPENDIX 2

We assume as α the weight to be attributed to the consumption S of the social group g. The present value of the net benefit for such a group will be

$$NB_g = \alpha_g(B_g - C_g) = \alpha_g dS_g \tag{A6}$$

and the total net benefit will be

$$NB = \sum_{g=1}^{G} \alpha_g dS_g. \tag{A7}$$

If it were possible to know the value of β in (A5), this value should be used as a substitute for α, and this would constitute the shadow price for taking distributional aspects into account. Nevertheless it is necessary to point out that a universally accepted objective measure of β_g does not exist, since this coefficient implies an underlying value judgement of the merit of the consumption of g.

3. Information Precision and Multicriteria Evaluation Methods

G. Munda, P. Nijkamp and P. Rietveld

1 EVALUATION AND POLICY MAKING

Evaluation aims at rationalizing planning and decision problems by systematically structuring all relevant aspects of policy choices (for instance, the assessment of impacts of alternative choice possibilities). Evaluation is usually not a one-shot activity, but takes place in all phases of decision making (for instance, on the basis of learning principles). In addition, a systematic support to complex planning and decision problems requires a balanced treatment, in order to avoid too much detail and too little information. Besides, the results of an evaluation procedure have to be transferred to environmental and regional policy makers in a manageable and communicable form, particularly because the items of an evaluation problem are usually multidimensional in nature (including incommensurable or even intangible aspects). Finally it has to be realized that the planning environment is usually highly dynamic, so that judgements regarding the political relevance of items, alternatives or impacts may exhibit sudden changes, hence requiring a policy analysis to be flexible and adaptive in nature. Rigid evaluation techniques run the risk of an evaluation not covering all issues of a regional, urban or transportation planning problem in a satisfactory way.

Any evaluation requires appropriate and balanced information, preferably based on meaningful and measurable indicators. The aims of an evaluation problem, however, are not always identical; they may be different and depend on actual institutional and administrative interests. Three broad categories of behavioural paradigms may be distinguished for public decision making: 'optimizing' behaviour, 'satisficing' behaviour and 'justifying' behaviour. Although the majority of formal evaluation techniques focus attention on the first category and, to a lesser extent, on the second category, in practice policy evaluation is often also used as a means of justifying policy decisions, even if the actual decisions are not in agreement with optimizing or satisficing principles.

Evaluation already has a long history covering more than 50 years. The history of plan and project evaluation before the Second World War showed, first, a strong tendency towards a financial trade-off analysis. Later on, much attention was focused on cost-effectiveness principles. After the Second World War, cost–benefit analysis gained increasing popularity in public policy evaluation. Several limitations inherent in cost–benefit analysis were eased by introducing amendments such as the planning balance sheet approach and the shadow project approach. The hypotheses underlying all these methodologies took for granted rational choice behaviour based on a one-dimensional, well defined performance indicator. The use of such conventional optimization models has been criticized from many sides. They often incorporate many limitations: the decision makers' indifference curves may involve local optima; incomplete or partial models may lead to inferior solutions; various objectives may be mutually conflicting; the level of measurement of one or more objectives may be imprecise; and so forth.

This unidimensional welfare approach implicitly assumes a perfectly competitive system: characterized by full information and a fully operating price system; conditions which can hardly be met in practice. Even if they can be fulfilled, many essential and policy-relevant elements of human life or human welfare cannot be translated into a common denominator, whether money or not. Consequently not only monetary consequences but also unpriced impacts of policy decisions have to be taken into account.

The increasing awareness of negative external effects of economic growth and the emergence of distributional issues in economic development have led to a need for more appropriate analytical tools for analysing conflicts between policy objectives. Multiple criteria evaluation techniques aim at providing such a set of tools. The main feature of these techniques is the simultaneous consideration of many (often conflicting) evaluation criteria (see Nijkamp et al., 1990).

In the past decades, the degraded state of the natural environment has become another key issue, and it is increasingly taken for granted that environmental and resource problems generally have far-reaching economic and ecological aspects or consequences. This implies that such problems are characterized, inter alia, by social, psychological, physicochemical and geological aspects. Such problems can therefore be used as useful examples of the complexities of much current policy analysis.

Models aiming at structuring these cross-boundary problems of an economic and ecological nature are often called 'economic–ecological' models (see Braat and Van Lierop, 1987). Since the complexity of this type of problem is high, models offering a comprehensible and operational representation of a real-world environmental situation are therefore very appropriate. The strong quantitative tradition in economics has enabled us to include environmental elements fairly easily in conventional models. Nevertheless, in integrating economic and environmental models, we also face some methodological problems, such as differences in time scales, differences in spatial scales and differences in measurement levels of the variables.

In environmental and resource policy making the following three main types of policy objectives can be distinguished: (1) nature conservation objectives, that is, 'minimum exploitation of natural systems', 'optimum yield'; (2) socioeconomic objectives, that is, 'maximum production of goods and services at minimum (private and social) cost'; (3) mixed objectives, that is, 'maximum sustainable use of resources and environmental services'. In economic–ecological evaluation models, socioeconomic and nature conservation objectives are considered simultaneously and, hence, multicriteria methods are a very appropriate modelling tool. Furthermore economic–ecological problems may be included in a general class of social systems, that is problems in which human beings play a central role. Generally such systems are of a large-scale type, characterized by a large number of variables and feedback loops. System science can help in structuring and modelling social problems, since it allows us to take into consideration the great number of data, relations and objectives that characterize such problems. This leads to the notion of concerted planning and evaluation methods, in which an attempt is made at designing and using multidimensional judgement methods for a variety of different policy criteria or objectives.

2 EVALUATION AS A PART OF PLANNING

Evaluation may be considered as a continuous activity which constantly takes place during a planning process. Even a limitation to a specific kind of evaluation does not change this characteristic, since there are always many choice possibilities during a planning process which have to be assessed and judged. However, for reasons of clarity, in this chapter we will restrict the meaning of the notion 'evaluation process' to a coherent set of distinct and policy-relevant alternatives. A simultaneous consideration of all relevant aspects is important here in order to denote that an evaluation process treats a planning component (for example, the evaluation of traffic circulation plans, the evaluation of alternative highway routes, or the evaluation of implementation schemes for physical planning) on the basis of multiple angles. It is noteworthy that evaluation processes have a cyclic nature. By 'cyclic nature' is meant the possible adaptation of elements of the evaluation resulting from continuous consultations between the various parties involved in the planning process at hand. The degree of complexity of an evaluation process depends on, among others, the evaluation problem treated, the time and knowledge available and the organizational context (see Nijkamp, 1990).

Generally an evaluation process will have the following structure (see Figure 3.1). It starts with a definition of what has to be evaluated (step 1). Next, various alternatives must be defined (step 2); this may be very easy (for instance, in the case of location decisions where regions or zones have to be evaluated), but sometimes it may be very difficult (as with the definition of policy alternatives) and in that case much attention should be paid to the procedure by which those alternatives are generated. So-called continuous evaluation methods (such as programming techniques) may then be appropriate, especially in connection with simulation models.

In addition the relevant evaluation criteria based on the above mentioned indicators have to be defined (step 3). These criteria can be used as a guideline for the analysis of the alternatives (step 4). For instance, if for an evaluation of transportation schemes several criteria have been formulated with respect to environmental issues, this may result, firstly, in a special environmental investigation of alternatives and, secondly, in an in-depth analysis of the aspects treated by the specific criteria. However practical

Figure 3.1 The structure of an evaluation process

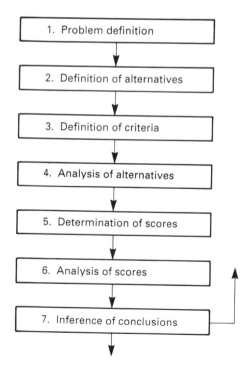

applications of multicriteria analysis show that this efficiency- and effectiveness-increasing relationship between step 4 and step 3 is not always envisaged. In this context, multiple criteria evaluation can be very helpful in structuring the research so that redundant analysis may be avoided

On the basis of the investigation of step 4, in step 5 the criterion (or impact or effect) scores can be determined, so that an evaluation matrix (or sometimes more than one) can be constructed. In the next step these scores have to be analysed (step 6). This can be done by simply comparing the alternatives for each criterion and by listing for each criterion the strong or weak alternatives, or by applying discrete multicriteria techniques. In the latter case, criterion priorities often have to be defined, because otherwise the information from the evaluation matrix cannot be amalgamated.

In the last step, 7, of Figure 3.1 conclusions have to be drawn and recommendations have to be prepared for the client (decision maker and so on). It is obvious that in this evaluation process, as outlined in Figure 3.1, many feedback loops may be recognized. Such feedback loops are a necessary ingredient in concerted planning and evaluation analysis.

In the light of the previous remarks, a concerted planning evaluation methodology may be represented as follows (see Figure 3.2), which can be seen as the envelope in which the elements of Figure 3.1 are components.

Figure 3.2   A systematic representation of a concerted planning evaluation methodology

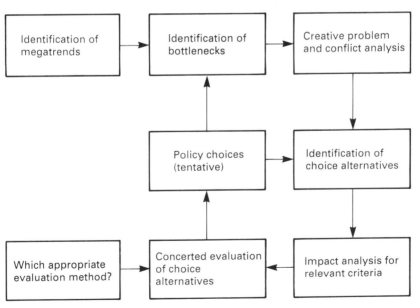

Questions are left unanswered in this scheme: what are the distinguishing features of multicriteria evaluation methods and which specific evaluation method has to be used for which planning problem? This will be discussed further in subsequent sections.

3 IDENTIFICATION OF APPROPRIATE MULTIPLE CRITERIA METHODS

In the 1970s and the early 1980s, a veritable avalanche of multiple criteria methods occurred, so that nowadays there is a wide variety of multiple criteria decision methods. These methods are not only used in the context of conventional project and plan evaluation, but also as an operational framework for conflict analysis in a concerted planning endeavour (for example, town planning, environmental management, regional planning, transportation planning).

The following reasons may be mentioned for the increasing popularity of these methods:

a. the impossibility of including intangible and/or incommensurable effects in conventional evaluation methods (like cost–benefit and cost-effectiveness analysis);
b. the conflictual nature of modern planning problems so that, instead of a single decision maker, various (often multi-level) formal and informal decision agencies determine a final choice in a particular context;
c. the shift from conventional 'one-shot' decision making to institutional and procedural decision making where a variety of strategic and opportunistic policy aspects play a role;
d. the desire in modern decision making not to be confronted with single unambiguous and (sometimes) imposed solutions, but with a spectrum of open feasible solutions, each having its own merits.

All these reasons have led to the current popularity of multiple criteria analysis in public planning. These methods can be used for different purposes and in different contexts. The following distinctions can be made regarding the contents and scope of multiple criteria evaluation methods:

1. *discrete versus continuous methods*: discrete evaluation methods focus attention on a finite set of (*a priori*) known) choice alternatives, whereas continuous evaluation methods are, in principle, related to a non-countable (and hence not precisely identifiable) set of choice alternatives;

2. *multi-person versus single-person evaluation*: in case of multi-person (or multi-committee) evaluation problems, it is in general impossible to assume unambiguous and *a priori* known trade-offs, so that flexibility allowing for dynamic preference articulation and bargaining procedures has to be ensured; for a single-person case it is often easier to specify policy priorities;
3. *identification versus selection of alternatives*: in various evaluation problems it is only necessary to identify a limited set of reasonable (or 'satisficing') choice possibilities, whereas in other cases the demands are put much higher: the unambiguous selection of a single alternative; in the first case, it may be sufficient to find a set of non-dominated (or Pareto) solutions for which the value of one policy objective cannot be improved without reducing the value of competing criteria;
4. *single-step versus multi-step evaluation procedures*: single-step evaluation takes for granted that a given evaluation problem must be solved immediately, whereas multi-step evaluation assumes a process character in evaluation (learning mechanisms, adaptive processes and so on);
5. *soft versus hard information*: soft evaluation problems are characterized by non-metric information (for example, ordinal data, qualitative statements), whereas hard problems are based on quantitative (for example, cardinal) information; an intermediate case is *mixed* information, which includes both qualitative and quantitative information. Such measurements issues will be discussed in the next section.

4 INFORMATION PRECISION AND UNCERTAINTY

In the modelling of a real-world problem, the first phase is to structure this problem. This phase depends above all on the available information; in fact the model must fit reality and not vice versa! Therefore a flexible model able to take into account the possible different types of information is of fundamental importance.

In the light of these observations, this chapter will address the issue of information precision and uncertainty. As is known from measurement theory (see Roberts, 1979), in structuring a problem, given a set A and some information about this set, there 'is a need to express this information by assigning to each element $a \in A$ a real number $m(a)$. This real number is called the measure of a and the application $m:A$---$>R$ is called a *scale of measurement*. The main scales of measurement are nominal scale, ordinal scale, interval scale and ratio scale. For simplicity, we will refer to qualitative information as information measured on a nominal or ordinal scale, and to quantitative information as information measured on an interval or ratio scale.

It has been argued that the presence of qualitative information in evaluation problems concerning socioeconomic and physical planning is a rule, rather than an exception. Thus there is a clear need for methods taking into account qualitative information. In multicriteria evaluation theory a clear distinction is made between quantitative and qualitative methods. Essentially there are two approaches for dealing with qualitative information: a direct and an indirect one. In the direct approach, qualitative information is used directly in a qualitative evaluation method; in the indirect approach, qualitative information is first transformed into cardinal information and then one of the existing quantitative methods is used. Cardinalization is especially attractive in the case of available information of a 'mixed type' (both qualitative and quantitative data). In this case, the application of a direct method would usually imply that only the qualitative part of all available (quantitative and qualitative) information is used, which would give rise to inefficiency. In the indirect approach, this loss of information is avoided; the question is, of course, whether there is a sufficient basis for the application of a certain cardinalization scheme.

Another problem related to the available information is the one of uncertainty contained in this information. Ideally, the information should be precise, certain, exhaustive and unequivocal, but, in reality, it is often necessary to use information which has not those characteristics and therefore to face the uncertainty of a stochastic and/or fuzzy nature present in the data. In fact, if the available information is insufficient or delayed, it is impossible to establish exactly the future state of the problem faced, so that then a *stochastic uncertainty* is created. Another type of uncertainty derives from the ambiguity of this information, since in the majority of the particularly complex problems involving men, much of the information is expressed in linguistic terms, so that it is essential to come to grips with the fuzziness that is either intrinsic or informational, typical of all natural languages. Therefore the combination of the different levels of measurement with the different types of uncertainty have to be taken into consideration. The taxonomy shown in Table 3.1 may be useful.

Table 3.1   Possible combinations of information measurement levels and uncertainty

	Quantitative information	*Qualitative information*
Certainty		
Uncertainty		

Stochastic uncertainty has been thoroughly studied in probability theory and statistics. *Fuzzy uncertainty* does not concern the happening of an event but the event itself, in the sense that it cannot be described unambiguously. This situation is very common in human systems. Spatial systems in particular are complex systems characterized by subjectivity, incompleteness and imprecision. Zadeh (1965) writes: 'as the complexity of a system increases, our ability to make a precise and yet significant statement about its behaviour diminishes until a threshold is reached beyond which precision and significance (or relevance) become almost mutually exclusive characteristics' (incompatibility principle). Therefore in these situations such statements as 'the quality of the environment is good', 'the unemployment rate is low' are quite common. Fuzzy set theory is a mathematical theory for the modelling of such situations, in which traditional modelling languages which are dichotomous in character and unambiguous in their description cannot be used. In the next section we will pay more specific attention to the use of fuzzy set elements in policy evaluation. A more formal presentation of these elements is contained in the Appendix to this chapter.

5 REPRESENTATION OF QUALITATIVE INFORMATION BY MEANS OF FUZZY SET THEORY

Traditionally the problem of representation of ordinal information in decision analysis has been treated by utility theory; for instance, when a subject has to choose one painting from ten, Luce and Raiffa (1989) propose the following procedure: 'We will present these to you in pairs and you will tell us which one of each pair you would prefer to own. After you have given your answers to all paired comparisons, we will actually choose a pair at random and present you with the choice you have previously made. Hence, it is to your advantage to record, as best as you are able, your own true tastes.' Therefore, if for all possible triples of alternatives the condition of transitivity is always satisfied, it is possible to make an ordinal ranking of feasible alternatives. Clearly the main assumptions of this approach are that the decision maker is always rational and consistent and that his preferences are always transitive in nature. Simon (1983) notes that humans have at their disposal neither the facts, nor the consistent structure of values, nor the reasoning power needed to apply the principles of utility theory. Therefore he presents as an alternative a 'behavioural model', maintaining that rational decision making basically involves the application of a certain range of personal values to resolve fairly specific problems a person faces, in a way that is satisfactory for that person.

Human judgements, especially in linguistic form, appear to be plausible and natural representations of cognitive observations. Psychological researches represent the cognitive process in the chain of transformations (see, for example, Freksa, 1982) shown in Figure 3.3.

Figure 3.3   Chain of transformations

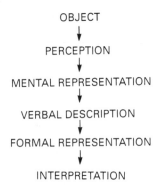

Very little is actually known about the first two transformations, and therefore it is more appropriate to concentrate our attention on the third (verbal description). Freksa (1982) writes:

> The distortion of information introduced in the third transformation appears to depend on the type of verbalization that is used. Numerical verbalization seems to let rather precise observations appear imprecise in many observers, while linguistic verbalizations seem to preserve more information from these observers. We can explain this phenomenon by *cognitive distance*. A linguistic representation of an observation may require a less complicated transformation than a numerical representation, and therefore less distortion may be introduced in the former than in the latter. We could say that the linguistic representation is cognitively closer to the mental description than the numerical representation.

In traditional mathematics, variables are assumed to be precise, but when we are dealing with our everyday language, imprecision usually prevails. Intrinsically, everyday language cannot be precisely characterized on either the syntactic or semantic level. Therefore a word in such language can technically be regarded as a fuzzy subset.

The previous observations lead to the conclusion that there is a wide variety of different methodologies and techniques for multicriteria evaluation. Now the question is: can we design a systematic filtering and screening method for the use of these methods? This will now be discussed.

6 TYPOLOGICAL APPROACH TO EVALUATION METHODS

Various classifications of multidimensional evaluation methods may be made. In the rest of this chapter we will employ the following typology: discrete multiple criteria methods versus continuous multiple objective methods, and hard information methods versus soft information methods. Consequently the typology seen in Table 3.2 can be created. In the literature on multiple criteria analysis most attention has been devoted to categories I and II (cf. Nijkamp *et al.*, 1990). Well known cardinal discrete methods of type I are: trade-off analysis, expected value method, concordance analysis and goals achievement method. Trade-off analysis is essentially a method for selecting the best alternative to achieve a prespecified benefit, given an unambiguous criterion (money, time, and so on). The existence of an unambiguous criterion makes it possible to compare expected gains with expected losses when considering the shift from one alternative to another.

Table 3.2   A typology of multidimensional evaluation methods

	Cardinal information	*Qualitative information*	*Mixed information*
Discrete multiple criteria methods			
Continuous multiple objective methods			

The expected value method assigns a set of weights to criteria and treats these weights as quasi-probabilities which add up to 1. Thus the expected value of the outcomes of each alternative can be calculated by multiplying the outcome (one for each criterion) by its appropriate weight and then by adding up the various parts. Concordance analysis is a widely used multiple criteria analysis based on a pairwise comparison of alternatives. This method measures the degree to which the alternative's outcomes and preference weights confirm or contradict the dominant pairwise relationships among alternatives. Finally the goals achievement method is a technique which relates objectives to quantitative achievement levels. To each criterion is assigned an index of relative importance. Then for each alternative outcome an achievement index is calculated, on the basis of which an aggregate achievement index for each plan is determined.

The following optimization models are well known cardinal continuous methods of category II: utility models, penalty models, goal programming models, min–max models and ideal point models. Utility models are based on the assumption that the whole vector of relevant objectives can be translated through a weighting procedure into the master control of one unambiguous utility function. Thus it presupposes *a priori* known trade-offs. Penalty models assume the existence of a set of desired achievement levels (that is, ideal vector), so that any discrepancy between an actual value and an ideal value is penalized by means of a penalty function. Goal programming models are among the most frequently used optimization models. They are essentially a subclass of penalty models, where both over- and underachievement of ideal values are taken into account during the optimization process.

Min–max models are based on the use of a pay-off matrix for conflicting objectives. When there are multiple objective functions (for instance, in the case of many participants, each with his objective function) the first step is a separate optimization with regard to each individual objective function. On the basis of the optimal value of each objective function a pay-off table representing the conflicts between the successive objectives can be constructed. Each column of this pay-off table pertains to a given objective function and each row pertains to a given strategy. In addition, an equilibrium solution for such a pay-off table can be identified: the solution which is nearest to the set of final solutions presented on the main diagonal of the pay-off table. Finally a related class of models, ideal point models, may be mentioned. They are based on a distance metric for the deviation between ideal solutions on the one hand and a set of efficient solutions on the other hand. A compromise solution is characterized by minimum distance between the ideal solution and one point from the set of efficient solutions.

Despite the large number of (simple and sophisticated) multiple criteria decision methods that are currently available, there is still surprisingly little insight into the conditions under which these models can best be applied. Therefore the present section will focus particularly on the question: which multiple criteria method is suitable for which class of conflict analysis? In this context, it is plausible to use a typological approach to classify multiple criteria decision methods on the basis of the features of different activities, of specified effects of these activities, and of the institutional planning and policy structure of the planning problem at hand. By including problem and procedure characteristics in large matrices, a classification and sequential selection of multiple criteria methods may then be carried out. The present chapter will draw on this approach and, in so doing, present a general conceptual typology of multiple criteria decision methods.

The typology presented here is primarily developed for decisions made by various kinds of governmental decision makers, but it may in principle also be useful for decisions to be taken in the private sector. Conflict management problems are in this chapter characterized according to two dimensions: the activity profile and the decision profile.

The Activity Profile

The activity profile can be characterized by two aspects: the activity type, and the type of effects caused by the activity. For example, a conflict-generating activity (being a stimulus in the form of a public decision) may be a project (such as the construction of a bridge), a plan (for example, a physical plan for urban renewal) or some form of public regulation from a government (the establishment of environmental standards for instance). There are numerous ways to classify the effects of such activities. Effects can be differentiated according to their temporal, spatial and other characteristics. An effect may be unique, repetitive, continuous short-term and continuous long-term. It may also be stationary or mobile, and/or within or outside the boundaries of the decision unit involved. An effect may be equally or unequally distributed over the parties involved. An effect may be compensatory (that is, the gains of the winners are sufficient to compensate the losers) or non-compensatory. And, finally, an effect may be submitted to formal standards or not.

The Decision Profile

Decision profile characteristics can be subdivided into the solution space and the decision space. The solution space comprises the alternatives set and information features. For example, the alternatives set may be composed of one, few or many alternatives, or it may be a continuous set. Information available regarding the conflict problem may be quantitative, qualitative or mixed. It may also be certain, uncertain with a known probability distribution or uncertain with an unknown probability distribution. Finally information may be limited or extensive, agreed or not agreed. The decision space comprises institutional characteristics, characteristics of decision makers, characteristics of required decision results (such as efficiency) and available means for the decision-making process.

In terms of institutional characteristics, for example, the decision may be based on one or multiple objectives, may involve two, three or more parties, and one or more decision levels. The decision procedure may be hierarchical or participatory and may be influenced by external interest groups. Finally a distinction can be made between routine and non-routine decisions. In terms of characteristics of decision makers, they can have an analytical or heuristic attitude, can be optimizers or satisfiers, can be short term-oriented, and risk-lovers or risk-averters (for a systematic presentation see also Table 3.3).

Now the problem of using the most appropriate evaluation method in concerted planning can be solved by identifying from the set of available methods the one that has a maximum agreement with the planning problem under consideration (see Table 3.4). We will now illustrate the use of one particular method for a given (qualitative) choice problem.

7 ILLUSTRATION OF A QUALITATIVE EVALUATION PROBLEM

Suppose that there are three possibilities for improving the transportation system in a region: highway construction, a road/bus system and a new train (railroad) system. Each of these three alternatives will be judged on the basis of five criteria: costs, travel time, capacity, nitrogen oxide emissions and landscape impacts. Some of these impacts are cardinal, but others are qualitative in nature. Furthermore we assume that all weights related to these criteria are qualitative. The impact (or effect) matrix related to ,the above problem is supposed to be as shown in Table 3.5 (see also Janssen, 1991):

Given this information of a mixed (quantitative/qualitative) type, there is a need to apply a multicriteria method suitable for such information. An interesting method for dealing with mixed information is the so-called 'regime' method (see Nijkamp et al., 1990). To some extent regime analysis can be interpreted as an ordinal generalization of pairwise comparison methods such as concordance analysis. Its point of departure is an ordinal evaluation matrix and an ordinal weight vector. Given the ordinal nature of the evaluation criteria, by means of pairwise comparison of alternatives, no attention is paid to the size of the difference between the impacts of alternatives; it is only the sign of the difference that is taken into account. Ordinal weights are interpreted as originating from unknown quantitative weights. A set S is defined containing the whole set of quantitative weights that conform to the qualitative priority information. In some cases the sign will be the same for the whole set S, and the alternatives can be ranked accordingly. In other cases the sign of the pairwise comparison cannot be determined unambiguously. This difficulty is circumvented by partitioning the set of feasible weights so that for each subset of weights a definite conclusion can be drawn about the sign of the pairwise comparison. The distribution of the weights within S is assumed to be uniform and therefore the relative sizes of the subsets of S can be interpreted as the probability that alternative a is preferred to alternative b. Probabilities are then aggregated to produce an overall rating of the alternatives, based on a success index or success score.

Table 3.3 Activity and decision profile of a compound decision problem

The method minimizes the chances of the worst results

The method maximizes the chances of the best results

The method allows for the introduction of constraints

The method is able to produce compromise solutions

The method leads to converging solutions

The method gives insight into the distribution of effects over the interested parties

The method produces efficient solutions

The method produces immediate results

The method is able to process uncertain information

The method is able to handle qualitative or mixed information in an efficient way

The method is able to handle quantitative information in an efficient way

The method is based on a decision function for discrete choices

The method is based on a continuous decision function

Given planning problem

Conflict management methods: selected set

1. concordance analysis
2. frequency method
3. lexicographic ranking
4. permutation method
5. eigenvalue method
6. regime method
7. multidimensional scaling
8. metagame method
9. mixed data method
10. trichotomic choice
11. score card method
12. key issue matrix
13. Delphi procedure
14. postponement of decision

Table 3.4 Confrontation of a requirement profile with a given planning problem

Attributes	Activity type	Activity profile – Type of effects			Solution space	
		Temporal	Spatial	Other	Alternative set	Information
Activity	project / plan / regulation; unique / repetitive	continuous short-term / continuous long-term; stationary / mobile	cross-boundary / within boundary; equal distribution / unequal distribution	compensatable / non-compensatable; formal standards / non-formal standards	one alternative / few alternatives / many alternatives / continuous	quantitative / quantitative mixed; certain / uncertain (probabilities known) / uncertain (probabilities not known)

Table 3.5 An impact matrix

Criteria	Units	Highway	Road/bus	Train	Weights
Costs	Millions of guilders	200	250	400	++
Travel time	---/+++	+++	++	+	+
Capacity	Millions of km/year	20	30	40	+++
Nitrogen oxide Emissions	ton/year	1000	750	100	+++
Landscape	---/+++	---	---	−	+

Note: The ---/+++ scale is interpreted as an ordinal scale.

By applying the regime method to the problem described above, the following matrix of relative pairwise success indices is obtained:

	Highway	Road/bus	Train
Highway	—	0.30	0.00
Road/bus	0.70	—	0.01
Train	1.00	0.99	—

Table 3.4 continued

Decision profile			
	Decision Space		
Institutional	Decision makers	Goal	Means

limited / extensive	agreed on / not agreed on	one objective / multi-objective	two parties / three parties or more	one decision level / multiple decision levels	participatory / hierarchical / interest groups	routine / non-routine	analytical / neuristic	optimizers / satisficers	short term-oriented / long term-oriented	risk-averter / risk-lover	one optimal alternative / set acceptable alternatives / ranking of alternatives	expertise / time / money / computer

From this it is clear that the train option is the preferable alternative, followed by road/bus and highway. The value 1.00 in the comparison between train and highway alternatives indicates that for this comparison no added value is to be expected from measurement of these criteria on a higher measurement scale. The probability that, given the ordinal information on travel time and landscape, the road/bus alternative ranks higher than the highway alternative equals 70 per cent.

A weak element in this approach is its one-shot nature; there is no scope for decision support as a coherent process. This will be discussed in the following section.

8 DECISION SUPPORT SYSTEMS FOR ENVIRONMENTAL PROBLEMS

Ginzberg and Stohr (1982) give the following definition of decision support systems (DSS): 'a DSS is a computer-based information system used to support decision making activities in situations where it is not possible or not desirable to use an automated system to perform the entire decision process'. Therefore the aim of a DSS is not to replace the decision maker but to help him during the evolution of a decision process, so that the focus is on the quality of the decision process rather than on the quality of the final decision.

The development of decision support systems reflects contributions from a variety of disciplines such as management science, computer science, economics, operations research, planning, psychology and geography. Such a variety of disciplines implies that it is very difficult to evaluate the quality of a DSS on the grounds of general principles, since qualities of a DSS are primarily shown by their usefulness in empirical applications to real-world problems. Environmental problems are complex owing to their multidimensional nature but also because of their temporal, spatial and institutional characteristics; these distinguish environmental decision making from other types of decision making and set specific demands for the support of these decisions.

These characteristics are related to the measurement level of the information, the time and spatial pattern of the effects and the number and type of participants in the decision problem. Therefore, in general in order to apply DSS in environmental problems successfully, the following properties may be mentioned (Janssen, 1991, p. 50):

1. *measurement level of information*: the characteristics of information require that a DSS deal adequately with non-monetary, qualitative and uncertain information;
2. *time pattern*: a DSS for environmental problems must be capable of including the specific time pattern of effects and must specifically be able to deal with a combination of short-term and irreversible effects;
3. *spatial pattern*: a DSS must be able to include spatial patterns of the effects in the decision;
4. *participants*: a DSS for environmental problems must be transparent to formal and informal participants in the decision process, available to all formal participants, provide adequate presentation of results and, finally, must make trade-offs explicit.

Of course, the construction of a DSS requires time and effort, and therefore the benefits in terms of increased effectiveness and efficiency of the availability of a DSS in a decision process need to be traded off against the costs of designing and implementing the system. Both benefits and costs depend on the complexity of the problem, the sophistication of the system and the subjective evaluation of people involved in the decision process.

9 CONCLUSION

Traditionally efficiency criteria such as income per capita have been used as major criteria to evaluate economic developments, welfare increases, growth perspectives and the social value of plans. During the last two decades it has been understood that welfare is a multidimensional variable which encompasses, inter alia, average income, growth, environmental quality, distributional equity, supply of public facilities and accessibility. Consequently not only monetary consequences but also unpriced impacts of policy decisions have to be taken into account. This implies that a systematic evaluation of public plans or projects has to be based on the distinction and measurement of a broad set of criteria. These criteria may be different in nature: private economic (investment costs, rate of return and so on), socioeconomic (for example employment, income distribution, access to facilities, etc.), environmental (pollution, deterioration of natural areas, noise), energy (use of energy, technological innovation, risk and so on), physical planning (for example as regards congestion, population density, accessibility) and so forth.

As a consequence, multicriteria evaluation techniques are an appropriate modelling tool. But in order to fit real-world problems, these methods must be able to treat the imprecision and uncertainty often present in the available information. It is not plausible to establish which method it is better to use in a given empirical problem *a priori*: the conditions under which these methods can best be applied are context-dependent, therefore the task is to choose the right method for the particular problem. In this context, a typological approach has been illustrated and some properties desirable for environmental DSS have been indicated.

BIBLIOGRAPHY

Braat, L.C. and Van Lierop, W.F.J. (eds.) (1987), *Economic–ecological Modeling*, Amsterdam: North-Holland.

Dompere, K.K. (1982), 'The theory of fuzzy decisions', in M.M. Gupta and E. Sanchez (eds), *Approximate Reasoning in Decision Analysis*, Amsterdam: North-Holland, pp. 365–79.

Freksa, C. (1982), 'Linguistic description of human judgements in expert systems and in the "soft sciences"', in M.M. Gupta and E. Sanchez (eds), *Approximate Reasoning in Decision Analysis*, Amsterdam: North-Holland, pp. 297–305.

Ginzberg, M.J. and Stohr, E.A. (1982), 'Decision support systems: issues and perspectives', in M.J. Ginzberg, W. Reitman and E.A. Stohr (eds), *Decision Support Systems*, Amsterdam: North-Holland.

Hoos, I. (1962), *Systems Analysis in Public Policy*, Berkeley: University of California Press.

Janssen, R. (1991), *Multiobjective Decision Support for Environmental Problems*, Amsterdam: PhD diss., Dept. of Economics, Free University.

Leung, Y. (1988), *Spatial Analysis and Planning under Imprecision*, Amsterdam: North Holland.

Luce, R.D. and Raiffa, H. (1989), *Games and Decisions*, New York: Dover.

Nijkamp, P. (1990), 'Environmental management methods and information precision' in A.G. Colombo and G. Premazzi (eds), *Indicators and Indices for Envi-*

ronmental Impact Assessment and Risk Analysis, Commission of the European Communities, EUR 13060 EN, pp. 235–56.

Nijkamp, P., Rietveld, P. and Voogd, H. (1990), *Multicriteria Evaluation in Physical Planning*, Amsterdam: North-Holland.

Roberts, F.S. (1979), *Measurement Theory with Applications to Decision Making Utility and the Social Sciences*, London: Addison-Wesley.

Simon, H.A. (1983), *Reason in Human Affairs*, Stanford: Stanford University Press.

Zadeh, L.A. (1965), 'Fuzzy Sets', in *Information and Control*, **8**, pp. 338–53.

APPENDIX: FUZZY SET THEORY

Fuzzy sets as formulated by Zadeh are based on the simple idea of introducing a degree of membership of an element with respect to some subsets. Let us assume that the symbol U means the entire set (universe of discourse). In classical set theory, given a subset A of U, each element $x \in U$ satisfies the condition: either x belongs to A, or x does not belong to A. The subset A is represented by a function $f_A: U \rightarrow [0, 1]$:

$$f_A(x) = \begin{cases} 1 & \text{if } x \in A \\ 0 & \text{if } x \notin A \end{cases}$$

The function f_A is called a characteristic function of the subset A. Fuzzy sets are then introduced by generalizing the characteristic function f_A. Let U again be a universe of discourse. Let $x \varepsilon U$. Then a fuzzy subset A in U is a set of ordered pairs

$$\{[x, \mu_A(x)]\}, \forall x \in U$$

where, $\mu_A: U \rightarrow M$ is a membership function which maps $x \varepsilon U$ into $\mu_A(x)$ in a totally ordered set M (called the membership set) and $\mu_A(x)$ indicates the grade of membership (degree of belonging) of x in A. Generally the membership set is restricted to the closed interval [0, 1]. A fuzzy set is completely determined by its membership function. For $0 < \mu_A(x) < 1$, x belongs to A only to a certain degree; thus there is ambiguity in determining whether or not x belongs to A. The physical meaning is that a gradual instead of an abrupt transition from membership to non-membership is taken into account. A classical example is that of age. Let U be the set of all non-negative integers. Let us take into consideration the primary terms 'young' and 'old'. These terms can be considered the label of two fuzzy sets A and B. No doubt the ages six or ten are young, whereas the ages 30 or 40 are less young. Thus it is possible to define a membership function μ_{Ayoung} showing the degree of compatibility of the age x to the concept of young.

It is indispensable, however to clarify here a point of fundamental importance: the use of membership functions. Membership functions constitute the essential basis on which the whole fuzzy set theory is built; they represent, no doubt, a brilliant idea which revolutionized traditional set theory, giving birth to a new mathematical field. But, paradoxically, the membership functions constitute at the same time the strongest and the weakest point of the theory.

Scientists are sometimes sceptical with regard to fuzzy sets, for the main reason that they consider these membership functions too subjective. Therefore it is necessary to address the question, on what factors does such a subjectivity depend? Two essential factors may be distinguished here: (1) the *context* in which they are to be applied; and (2) the *method* adopted in the building phase. We will now discuss these factors in more detail. The membership functions depend on the semantic contents of the subjective category they represent and therefore they vary according to the context in which they are to be applied. Then the question is whether this feature is really a negative one. In general, when an attempt is made to model a real-world situation, the presence of a certain subjective component appears to be an inevitable phenomenon. Models by definition only give a partial representation of reality. As a consequence there are usually many alternative model formulations possible. There are several criteria available to judge whether a model is an adequate representation of reality. The way these criteria are applied inevitably contains a subjective element, as a one-to-one mapping between model and reality is an illusion.

The second factor concerns the building phase. One way to build membership functions is to use deductive methods with the use of formal models constructed according to specific hypotheses. A second approach is empirical in nature. Here we can distinguish two cases: (1) interpolating a finite number of degrees of membership, and (2) constructing a real model of a membership function and seeking to verify its empirical validity. In our opinion, the empirical approach is more suitable for evaluation and decision models. Our position with respect to fuzzy set approaches in this context is that we regard the use of fuzzy sets as desirable – or even necessary in some cases – for three reasons:

1. it is possible to deal in a suitable manner with the ambiguity often present in available information;
2. it is possible to do more justice to the subjective or creative component of the individual decision maker;
3. it is possible to interact with a DSS in natural language by employing linguistic variables.

4. Cost–Benefit Analysis: Applied Welfare Economics or General Decision Aid?

Alan Williams

1 INTRODUCTION

Cost–benefit analysis is designed to help public bodies to make decisions (about the deployment of scarce resources) which will affect the welfare of those individuals in the community to which the public body is accountable. So before analytical work can begin, the analyst needs to know the context within which the choice is going to be made, the nature of the alternatives to be considered, the size and composition of the relevant community, and the objectives of the members of that community (that is, what it is that they value). Since most communities contain people who have different views on the matters affected by the collective choice in question, the analyst faces a further problem in deciding how these different views are to be aggregated; that is, about whose values are to count, and for how much, when the final balance is struck. Thus in the early stages of any cost–benefit study a dialogue needs to be conducted in which these matters are explored thoroughly by both the analyst and the 'client', so that all parties are clear from the outset what the terms of reference are, and why (see Munda *et al.*, above).

From this formulation of the choice situation it will be obvious that the relationship between the analyst (as a technical authority) and the decision maker (as a political authority) is an intimate one, so intimate indeed that in practice it is sometimes very difficult to disentangle the role of the one from the role of the other (see Pignataro, below). And in making that observation we are not simply thinking of the situations in which the analyst deliberately usurps the politician's role by injecting his or her own values into the analysis so as improperly to influence the outcome in a desired direction, or even of the converse situations in which the politician deliberately usurps the analyst's role by suppressing evidence so as improperly to influence the outcome in some other direction. Although these are problems (and very real problems) concerned with maintaining the integrity of policy analysis, what the earlier observation actually referred to was the difficulty, experienced even by people with integrity, in differentiating between matters which are properly 'technical' and matters which are properly 'contextual' (that is, political).

Although practical cost–benefit analysis had its origins in attempts by engineers to optimize public policy decisions about water resource development, it was soon seized upon by economists, critical of the lack of sophistication in what the engineers were doing. The economists then developed the methodology further within the general framework of Paretian Welfare Economics (see Battiato, above). The great advantage of this system of thought is that it enables economists to circumvent the problems associated with aggregating the changes in welfare experienced by different individuals. It does this by requiring as the basic information only each person's own judgement as to whether he or she is better off or worse off (or, on balance, the same as before) as a result of some specified change in their situation. The general rule is that, if such a change makes at least one person better off, and leaves nobody worse off, than that change is a 'Pareto improvement', and if the system reaches a situation in which it is impossible to make *anyone* better off without making someone else worse off, that situation is 'Pareto optimal'. Unfortunately 'Pareto improvements' have come to be labelled improvements in *efficiency*, and 'Pareto optimal' situations have come to be labelled *efficient* situations, and in the process the special assumptions that lie behind this persuasive shorthand have tended to become obscured.

There are, of course, very few real-world situations which would satisfy this rather strict general rule, so it was relaxed to include situations in which the potential gainers should compensate the potential losers and, if there were still some gains left after full compensation had been paid, then the new situation would once more be a Pareto improvement, for (after compensation had been paid) there would be at least one gainer and no losers. The new element required by this more relaxed rule is to determine how compensation is to be paid. The obvious medium is money, so it became necessary to estimate the value of the gains as the sum of money the gainers are willing to pay for them, and to estimate the value of the losses as what the losers would regard as adequate compensation for suffering them. If the former sum outweighed the latter sum, then by a suitable redistribution of the former sum a Pareto improvement could be ensured. Note that there is nothing in this formulation which requires gains or losses to be measured at market prices, or even for markets to exist for the 'goods' that are gained or lost (for example, beautiful views). All that is required is that the affected individuals can evaluate such gains or losses using money as a unit of measurement. (Munda *et al.* above, seem to take too narrow a view of the requirements of welfare economics here, apparently believing *not only* that markets are required *but also* that they must be perfectly competitive).

Here, however, some further weakening of the original criterion occurred, because the actual payment of compensation might be extremely costly to implement, so it was held that it would be sufficient for the purposes of analysis if it could be shown that a particular change represented a *potential* Pareto improvement. But although under this weaker rule it had to be shown that the gainers *could* compensate the losers, it was left to the policy makers to decide whether such compensation should actually be paid or not. So it became possible for a proposed change to be presented as 'efficient' even though some people would actually be worse off as a result. The possible harshness of this position with respect to the losers was held by some to be ameliorated by the fact that the public sector embarks on thousands of projects every year and, by the law of averages, if every one of them generates more gains than losses, then in the long run everyone will finish up being a net beneficiary. There are good reasons to doubt this.[1]

It is quite difficult to resist a proposal which has apparently been demonstrated to improve efficiency, yet there may be very good reasons for doing so in certain circumstances, and it is these circumstances that will be explored in this chapter. The material will be taken up in the following order: first of all the obvious equity issues about the distribution of gains and losses will be considered; secondly the methods used to value gains and losses will be examined; thirdly the conventional aggregation methods used in cost–benefit studies will be reviewed; and finally the nature of the dialogue required between analysts and decision makers will be given brief consideration. The purpose in each section will be to identify key assumptions sometimes made unconsciously by analysts, but which need to be brought into the open and explicitly judged (by the decision maker or by the relevant community) as appropriate or inappropriate in the particular context. Each section will start with the assumptions typically made by economists who work within the Paretian framework (which means by most economists). It will be concluded that, if cost–benefit analysis is to serve as a useful decision aid in a democratic society, those practising it must be prepared to cast off the Paretian strait jacket where necessary. A further conclusion will be that those commissioning such studies must be prepared to enter into a searching dialogue with the analyst about the contextual issues which have to be settled, and to be prepared to justify publicly whatever stance they take on them.

2 THE EQUITY–EFFICIENCY TRADE-OFF

The most frequently considered weakness in Paretian Welfare Economics is its alleged neglect of distributional (or equity) issues. In the simplest terms, when declaring a particular outcome an improvement it does not matter within the Paretian framework *who* is better off. It is all the same whether that person is already the best off person, or the worst off person, or a good or evil person, or in any other sense deserving or undeserving *in the eyes of others*. Each individual's welfare is to be judged solely by that individual, using whatever criteria that individual chooses to use. Moreover these judgements about changes in each individual's welfare are made from whatever initial position happens to be the actual starting-point for the analysis. No judgements are made about how 'equitable' or 'inequitable' the starting-point itself might be.

If equity judgements *are* appropriate in a particular context, then it is usually suggested that optimality be thought about in a two-dimensional way, in which one dimension will be 'efficiency' and the other will be 'equity'. If both are socially desirable goals, then we may well have to 'trade off' one against the other, for example sacrificing some efficiency in the interests of equity (or vice versa). There is some difficulty with this particular formulation of the problem, for it assumes that there is no equity judgement *within* the efficiency dimension. But there is. If by an equity principle we mean a principle of distributive justice, and if making judgements about distributive justice means making judgements as to whether one distribution of rights or rewards or responsibilities is more just than another, the Paretian judgement is essentially that the only relevant source of injustice is making someone worse off (in their own judgement). Provided *this* can be avoided, all is well. Thus we only need to think in terms of an 'efficiency–equity trade-off' if we wish to substitute some other equity principle for this one! It seems to me that such a trade-off might equally well be called an 'equity–equity' trade-off, for what is happening is that the Paretian position is being replaced by some other position (typically an egalitarian one of some kind or other).

It appears to be very difficult to formulate an equity principle to replace Pareto's that is as precise as Pareto's, so if distributional issues are held to be important many economists simply advocate *displaying* the gains and losses to different individuals or groups, and leaving the matter there for the decision makers (and/or their constituents) to sort out. This would be facilitated if separate (disaggregated) cost–benefit 'accounts' were presented, each of which represented the impact of the various alternatives as seen from one particular standpoint (see Munda *et al.*, above). Others take the view that testing the consequences of alternative views about distributive justice is too complex a task to be left entirely to the casual and informal methods of assessment typically used by decision makers (and/or by the members of the community they serve) and should remain within the analyst's remit. It will be argued shortly that, since there is already a great deal of concealed distributional weighting within the aggregation methods used by analysts it is probably better on balance for this aspect of the analysis to be an explicit part of their remit, even though some may see it as usurping of the role of the politicians. My view is that equity issues are more likely to be followed through explicitly and systematically if the analysts deal with them than if others do so, *but only if a much richer and fuller dialogue occurs at all stages in a study than is often the case at present.*

3 THE VALUATION OF GAINS AND LOSSES

As indicated earlier, the compensation principle, and the use of the potential Pareto criterion, have led to monetary valuations of gains and losses playing a central role in cost–benefit analysis. Since the readiest sources for such valuations are the markets in which goods and services are traded (both for consumer goods and for factor services), it is natural that these markets should be regarded as the first place to seek such information. It is rare, however, for such valuations to be used in their raw state in cost–benefit studies, for it is recognized that most markets are subject to considerable distortions due to lack of competition, tax subsidy measures, externalities (such as environmental pollution) and so on. But some important goods and services have no ready market at all (people's leisure time, peace and quiet, or clean air, for instance) so attempts have to be made to locate them in a chain of trade-offs which will eventually bring us to an item for which there is a market, and by that device a money valuation is derived indirectly for such non-traded goods and services. For instance, people seeking peace and quiet will tend to move into quieter neighbourhoods, so (other things being equal) relative house prices may give us a clue as to the 'premium' that they are willing to pay to avoid noise (or crime, or environmental pollution, or whatever else it might be).

There are considerable technical difficulties in eliciting some of these adjusted market valuations, but these difficulties are not our concern here.[2] Our emphasis is on the underlying assumptions involved in adopting this general stance on valuation issues, namely that individuals' willingness and ability to pay is the appropriate concept to be pursuing. It rests once more on the assumption that the underlying distribution of purchasing power is an acceptable basis on which to proceed, and that individuals are the best judges of their own welfare. There may be contexts in which either or both of these assumptions are not appropriate. We do not, for instance, allow votes in the elections for parliamentary representatives to be bought and sold, but instead we distribute them one per (adult) person, with no transfers permitted. In that context it would not seem appropriate to value the right to vote by people's willingness and ability to pay for such a right – indeed it might be quite misleading to do so, for the right to vote might be much more valuable to a poor person than to a rich one (who may have many other ways of securing what he or she needs). And in the case of children we do not regard them as the best judges of their own welfare, and hence regulate closely their income earning possibilities and their consumption possibilities, and require them to go to school whether they (or indeed their parents) wish it or not (though there may also be an element of social interest in this, in addition to any desire to promote the child's own interests in a paternalistic way).

These two elements (the rejection of the existing distribution of income as an appropriate starting-point, and scepticism as to whether people are necessarily always the best judges of their own welfare) combine when it comes to the evaluation of health care (see Drummond, below). Most publicly provided health care has the explicit objective of offering access to health care irrespective of income or wealth, or indeed of any other consideration other than need, and although these lofty ideals are seldom achieved 100 per cent in practice, in such circumstances it would be wholly inappropriate to evaluate health care on the basis of individuals' willingness and ability to pay, for that would imply attaching more value to health care for the rich than to health care for the poor.

It is interesting to compare the situation that has developed with respect to studies of health care (see Drummond, below) with the situation that has developed with respect to transport studies (see Nash, below). In the transport field the most important element quantitatively is time saving, but, when it comes to accident prevention, health issues are also present. In the valuation of life in transport, both the value of lost output, and willingness and ability to pay to reduce the risks of accidents, have been prominent in cost–benefit studies. Clearly in this field no qualms are felt about letting the existing distribution of purchasing power influence the valuations, because access to the transport network is not regarded as something which should be an equal right for all citizens (as access to the ballot box is). It is rather seen as part of the reward system of the society, so that it is perfectly acceptable for the rich to have bigger and better cars than the poor, or to be able to travel first class rather than second class on trains or planes. Nor does there seem to be any problem in the transport field about assuming that individuals are the best judges of their own welfare (except, again, for children). People are generally assumed to be competent in that respect, with a few notable exceptions such as requiring the wearing of seat belts in cars and the wearing of crash helmets by motorcyclists. Most of the other apparently 'paternalistic' departures from individuals' willingness and ability to pay as the fundamental source of valuations, seem mostly to be motivated by a concern for the welfare of others (for example, vehicle safety regulations, driving tests, alcohol testing). So it is not that the approach adopted in health care is 'right' and that adopted in transport is 'wrong' (or vice versa) but that each appears appropriate in its own context, but would be inappropriate in the other context.

Deciding that willingness and ability to pay is not, for one reason or another, a suitable basis of valuation in some specific context leaves us with the problem of deciding what to put in its place, since valuation *per se* cannot be avoided. Other possible sources of value might be the direct eliciting of trade-offs from people's utility functions, or the postulated values of the responsible politicians, or 'expert' judgements from the professionals in the relevant field! Each of these alternative sources of valuation has strengths and weaknesses, and the actual valuations that emerge might not be identical, which will bring to the fore the necessity for a political–ethical decision as to whose values shall count (of which more shortly). But these alternative methods will not necessarily yield valuations that are expressed in money terms, so we may have to move from a cost–benefit to a cost-effectiveness framework, in which benefits are measured not in terms of money but in 'natural' units (such as 'lives saved'). In principle this will still enable us to say which is the best of the alternatives under consideration, but it will prevent us from being able to say whether even the *best* of the alternatives under consideration is worth doing at all, since we cannot say whether the benefits outweigh the costs (since the benefits are in 'natural' units and the costs are in money units). To proceed further we would have to place a money value on the 'natural' unit itself (for example, to decide what level of cost is acceptable in order to save a life), which might well be achieved by simply making an explicit political judgement.

It is tempting to think that, by staying *within* the limitations of cost-effectiveness analysis, and simply adopting 'natural' units (such as lives saved) as the basis for benefit measurement (without attaching money values to them), all valuation problems can be avoided. There is a hint of this in the multicriteria approach. But this is an illusion. For instance, in clinical trials in medicine it is common to use the survival rate over some arbitrarily chosen time period as the measure of effectiveness (or benefit) and by this criterion to assert that one treatment is better than another. But if we examine more closely what is involved here (say with the two-year survival rate) we will find that it carries the following implicit *valuation* statements:

1. to survive for less than two years is of no value;
2. having survived two years, further survival is of no additional value;
3. it does not matter with what *quality* of life people survive to two years;
4. it does not matter who you are (every survivor counts equally).

These are very strong valuation assumptions. They can be modified by adopting a different measure such as life years gained, or, better still, quality-adjusted life years gained, but whatever unit is used there are some implicit valuation statements to be teased out and exposed.

Health economists have tried to bridge the gap between these 'natural' units and full-scale monetary evaluation by attempting to elicit people's preferences, and even the properties of their underlying utility functions, in what has become known as the cost–utility approach – as opposed to the cost-effectiveness or cost–benefit approach (see Drummond, below). This has generated considerable tension between the economists (and a few others) who are trying to create a *single index of value of health*, using psychometric methods, and those (mostly epidemiologists and sociologists) who believe this to be an impossible (and even a politically dangerous and/or ethically indefensible) undertaking, and who would prefer to leave the cost-effectiveness framework operating with multiple criteria of success, with no trade-offs between them. This same tension is also clearly evident in the field of environmental protection, where the use of the multicriteria approach has come to dominate the analytical scene (see Munda *et al.*, above).

Thus in this approach 'life years gained' might be one criterion and 'improvements in quality of life' another, but it would not be considered proper to try to establish the rate at which people might be willing to sacrifice life expectancy to improve their quality of life, or vice versa. This 'profile' (or multicriteria) approach, in which several distinct indicators of effectiveness are displayed, is fine if the different indicators do not contradict each other, and if only the *direction* (rather than the size) of the differences in benefit is required in order to make a decision (for example, if you were committed to spending a certain sum of money on an activity willy-nilly, and you simply wanted to know which course of action is *more* beneficial). These are very restrictive conditions, however, and greatly emasculate the scope for using such appraisal methods. What typically happens within them is that trade-offs are introduced informally and subjectively during the decision making process, thus escaping both public scrutiny and rigorous analysis of their implications. Munda *et al.*, above, see the desire, in modern decision making, for the analyst to present a spectrum of open feasible solutions, each with its own merits, as one of the reasons for the increased popularity of multicriteria methods. But this popularity should be suspect if it is due to the fact that politicians prefer to maximize their scope for

Cost–Benefit Analysis: Applied Welfare Economics or General Decision Aid 73

injecting their own *implicit* weights into the analysis, in a context in which these are not exposed to public scrutiny and hence for which they cannot be held accountable. Worse still, if these weights are not made explicit to the analysts either, their implications will not be systematically explored and in complex situations they may have quite different implications for policy from those that the politicians believe them to have.

Thus, in general terms, the decisions about what to include and what to exclude and the decisions about which valuation method to employ must not be regarded simply as technical matters for the experts to decide on, because they are also matters on which a judgement has to be made about what is (politically) appropriate or inappropriate in the particular context of the study. But this 'political' judgement should not be arbitrary, or presented *ex cathedra* without argument or justification, for that would be contrary to the purpose of cost–benefit analysis, which is to be both explicit and systematic about the factors involved in the particular choice under investigation.[3]

4 AGGREGATION: FROM INDIVIDUALS TO THE COLLECTIVITY

Since the decision on which the analysis is focusing is a collective one, yet it is assumed to be responsive, in some ill-defined way, to the views of the individuals in the community to whom the decision maker is accountable, it becomes of crucial importance to be clear about whose values count (and for how much) in the valuation process, and how the basic units of benefit or cost are added together.

The typical way of doing this is to take an average value as the group value (for instance as is done with the value of time in transport studies). But an average (more precisely, an arithmetic mean) is not the only measure of central tendency available to an analyst. There are the geometric mean, the mode and the median, to mention but three. There is a tendency to regard the selection of the appropriate measure of central tendency as a technical matter which, by convention, would be influenced strongly by the convenience of its mathematical properties and by the nature of the distribution of the particular set of values it seeks to encapsulate in a single number. Of course it is not necessary to use *only* the measure of central tendency to summarize the properties of a whole distribution of values, for alongside each such measure there is an associated measure of the spread of the distribution (such as the variance or the interquartile range) and even of the skewness of the distribution. But these technical matters are not our concern here. What *is* our concern is the implication of any particular selected measure for *whose views count* (and for how much).

Let us take a simple example in which the distribution of values across seven individuals is 2, 3, 3, 6, 8, 10, 108. The mode is 3, the median is 6, and the arithmetic mean is 20. It clearly makes a big difference which measure of central tendency is used! But let us look at the matter as if *each individual is casting a vote*. Choosing to use the *mode* is equivalent to putting each of the six different values (2,3,6,8,10 and 108) to a vote, and choosing the one that gets the most votes. Choosing to use the *median* is equivalent to taking the person in the middle of the rank ordering of values as the representative person for the group. Choosing to use the *arithmetic mean* assigns people different weights according to the values they express, so that the person on the high extreme gets more weight than the person at the low extreme (in this particular case, indeed, more weight than everyone else put together). With a symmetrical compact distribution of values these differences would not arise, so the aggregation problem is not always as severe in its implications as in our numerical example, but the fact remains that the choice of measure of central tendency has possible political implications which require it to be justified in a manner which is not just technical. In a two-party system working by simple majority voting on one issue at a time, it is the median voter who is pivotal and whose views are therefore likely to be the most important for collective decision making, rather than the view represented by taking the arithmetic mean of the distribution. Political considerations lurk in the most unexpected places!

5 DIALOGUE

When a project is selected and formulated for analysis, it is relatively rare for the process from which it has emerged to be as rigorous and well structured as that described by Munda *et al.*, above. It is much more common for a problem to emerge from rather haphazard, but unresolved, debate within a politico-bureaucratic process, in which the only thing the contending parties can agree about is that it might help to clarify the ongoing discussions to have a rather better factual basis to work on than they have at the moment. An exception to this general observation is the situation where a project appraisal system has become routine, as in some areas of transport investment (see Nash, below) but even here the original starting-point was as described above. In such an unstructured situation it is likely to be the analyst who needs to take the initiative in ensuring that the terms of reference within which the appraisal is to be conducted are likely to be both politically appropriate and analytically productive and, as will be argued shortly, these two criteria may prove to be at odds with each other.

The general injunction, 'think before you act', is as applicable to analysts as it is to decision makers, and time spent clarifying the precise purposes of a project, and how these relate to the general objectives of the organization, is seldom time wasted. It is also worth enquiring whether the project bears, directly or indirectly, on the objectives or activities of any other public body, and by what criteria any of the interested parties are likely to judge the outcomes from the alternatives under consideration. If distributional issues are likely to be important, it is also important to identify the particular subgroups in the population who will be the focus of such attention (for example, rich versus poor, or people in one locality versus those in another, or particular occupational groups, or consumers versus producers). The need to take such elements into consideration greatly complicates the study design, but such complications need to be taken into account at the outset, for it is usually even more difficult to take them into account effectively once a study is under way.

But the choice of alternatives to be appraised should not be taken for granted either. Typically they will have emerged from a filtering process in which the driving force will have been 'experts'. The professional backgrounds of the respective experts (be they engineers, doctors or bankers) will predispose them to seeking solutions along particular lines, but not along others. Their professional pride will also come into play, so they will not be happy with projects that fall short of what they regard as the 'current state of the art', and they will be anxious to promote projects that bring them professional prestige without too much regard to their costs. Possible solutions which do not meet these preconditions are therefore likely to have been removed from the scene at a much earlier stage. Moreover they and the decision makers may well have prior notions as to what sort of solution is likely to prove the most cost-effective (for example, one that is capital-intensive and saves labour) so only those sorts of solutions may be left in the competition. But it may be that the labour-saving solutions are heavy users of power, or of imported equipment, both of which have been informally undervalued during the selection process. For analytical purposes, it is better to have a wide range of options to consider which have very different characteristics than it is to have a careful selection which is vaguely believed to be the best (on the basis of the very imperfect information available to the parties prior to the appraisal). There may well be surprises in store once the analysts get to work!

As well as questioning the selection of broadly defined alternatives to be appraised, the detailed definition of each alternative also needs to be scrutinized carefully. The scale, timing and composition of the project's elements need to be challenged and, if necessary, sub-alternatives defined and analysed. It needs to be made clear whether the various alternatives are mutually exclusive or whether more than one might be accepted (see Mayston, above) and, if the latter, whether they are interdependent in any way (for example, in a comparison of road and rail links between two places, it would be possible to do both, but appraising the addition of a rail link to a road link is quite different from appraising a rail link in the absence of a road link). Time horizons may also be critical, and the longer they are the more pervasive are likely to be the uncertainties surrounding the context in which the completed project will be operating, creating further difficulties for the analyst.

One final set of contextual questions which tends not to be given enough attention when setting up problems for appraisal concerns the time and resources available. There are two sources of difficulty here. One is that the decision makers want the answers by yesterday, which makes good, thoughtful analysis difficult. This sense of urgency is often misplaced, and owes more to bureaucratic convenience than to the realities of the problem in hand. It is not that the underlying problem (for example, the site of the third London airport) has to be solved by a particular date (indeed, it still has not been solved 25 years on), but rather that in some timetable of events it would be more useful to have an answer by such-and-such a date than later on. This may lead to inadequate and misleading analysis, which is particularly serious for large, important, one-off decisions. The other source of difficulty is the exact opposite of this, namely when referring a problem for further study is regarded as a way of getting it off the political agenda for a while, and the people concerned have therefore no strong motivation to help the analysts get on with it at all.

For all these reasons it might be useful for anyone embarking on a piece of project appraisal to carry in his or her head the catechism of 'Twenty Questions' set out in the appendix to this chapter. Not all of them will necessarily be relevant in every case, but until you pursue them you will not know; and acting without thinking about them could prove extremely frustrating and costly, both at a personal and at a system level.

6 CONCLUSION

The general theme of this chapter has been that there are many conventional assumptions that are made by economists when conducting cost–benefit studies which some of them seen to believe to be purely technical matters forming an essential part of a value-free calculus concerned with making the public sector more efficient. Thoughtful practitioners of the art have long realized that this is not the true situation, and that the usual starting-point (which is normally Paretian Welfare Economics) is often very limited in its applicability and needs to be supplemented (or complemented) by drawing on other analytical foundations.

It is dangerous to have different analysts working in different ways with different data and then presenting conflicting (but non-comparable) conclusions, which have then to be resolved informally and obscurely by people who are not really aware of what has gone into the various analyses they are trying to digest. Preference is therefore given to the steady expansion of the scope of cost–benefit analysis by making it much more versatile than is possible from within the Paretian paradigm. But this expansion of scope means becoming more multidisciplinary, and in particular accepting, as legitimate sources of valuation, phenomena which lie outside markets and market-type choices. Cost–benefit analysis is then concerned with anything that people value (however they value it) and its purpose is to help ensure that the value of additional things that are provided by some project is greater than the value of the things that have to be sacrificed.

By becoming more versatile in this way, cost–benefit analysis also becomes more risky, because it is operating in a minefield of political and quasi-political issues which need to be exposed and circumnavigated with great care. Allan Schmid recently put the matter very clearly,[4] and to him will be left the last word:

> Analysis is ... a means for systematically implementing politically chosen objectives on the size and content of production and its distribution. Analysis should show decision makers the specific choices that follow from more generally stated preferences chosen from outside the analytic system... Systematic analysis allows observers to determine the objectives being pursued and whether these objectives are being pursued consistently or piecemeal over some chosen scope of application. The analysis should allow different groups with different interests to see how the government's proposed ... choices will affect them ... on the premise that good analysis will facilitate widespread, informed public participation in decision-making.

NOTES

1. Alan Williams, 'Income Distribution and Public Expenditure Decisions', in M. V. Posner (ed.), *Public Expenditure: Allocation between Competing Ends*, Cambridge: Cambridge University Press, 1977.
2. See Alan Williams, 'Cost-Benefit Analysis: Bastard Science and/or Insidious Poison in the Body Politick?', *Journal of Public Economics*, 1972, I(2), pp.199–226 (also reproduced in R. Haveman and J. Margolis, *Public Expenditure and Policy Analysis*, 2nd edn, 1977, pp. 519–49).
3. For a fuller account of these problems, and how they might be resolved, see R. Sugden and A. Williams, *The Principles of Practical Cost Benefit Analysis* Oxford: Oxford University Press, 1978.

4. A. Allan Schmid, *Benefit–Cost Analysis: A Political Economy Approach*, Boulder, Col.: Westview Press, 1989, p.3.

APPENDIX: TWENTY QUESTIONS ON THE THEME, THINK BEFORE YOU ACT!

1. What are the purposes of the project?
2. How do they relate to the general purposes of the organization?
3. Do they bear, directly or indirectly, on the objectives/activities of any other public body?
4. By what criteria are *any* of the interested parties likely to judge outcomes/alternatives?
5. Are distributional issues important?
6. Is the *widest* possible range of options being considered?
7. What filtering process has already been going on?
8. Are the different options technically mutually exclusive, or could more than one be accepted?
9. If more than one might be accepted, are they interdependent?
10. What variants of each broad strategic option might there be (for example, timing, scale or composition)?
11. What time horizon is appropriate to the problem?
12. What are the assumed contextual constraints?
13. Should any of them be relaxed for analytical purposes?
14. Do they hold over the whole time horizon of the project, or might they become more/less stringent as time goes by?
15. Is it worth setting up alternative scenarios within which to appraise the alternatives?
16. Who will be called upon to act on the outcome of the study?
17. Are they likely to want the results of the study to be presented in a particular way?
18. Is a common format likely to work for all parties, or will each need a different format?
19. What can be done to ensure that the different presentations can be systematically related to one another?
20. How much time/how many resources are available with which to do the appraisal?

PART II

Particular Applications

5. Cost–Benefit Analysis of Transport Projects

Chris Nash

1 INTRODUCTION

Transport was amongst the first fields in which cost–benefit analysis (CBA) came into regular application as a part of decision taking. For instance, in Britain two of the classic seminal applications of the technique were the studies of the M1 motorway (Beesley, Coburn and Reynolds, 1960) and of the Victoria Line – an underground railway line in London (Beesley and Foster, 1963). Following these studies, techniques were developed for the routine appraisal of road schemes and of public transport schemes where these have a social intent.

It is interesting to speculate as to why transport has proved such a fruitful area for application of the technique. Perhaps it is partly the fact that there are many fairly similar schemes to rank, so that a formalized appraisal system is more attractive than relying on the use of judgement. Perhaps it is that the major benefit of transport projects – time savings – is readily measured, and does not arouse the same hostility to monetary valuation as do the benefits of more sensitive schemes such as health projects. Whatever the reasons, the long history of transport project appraisal makes this application a good test of the value of the technique. If it is not helpful in this sector, it is unlikely to be anywhere!

In this chapter we first describe the basic methods of CBA of transport projects, illustrating them from current British Department of Transport practice, together with comment on the degree to which this approach differs from that commonly found elsewhere (these comments rest heavily on a recent survey by Sanderson, 1989). We then address some of the criticisms of the technique as commonly used. These concern the forecasting of traffic levels, the treatment of environmental, land use and development effects, the question of income distribution, the issue of comparability of appraisal methods between modes and the relationship between project appraisal and strategic choice. Following this, we turn briefly to alternative approaches to appraisal, including objectives-based and multicriteria techniques. Finally, we present our conclusions on the value of cost–benefit analysis of transport projects.

2 METHODOLOGY OF TRANSPORT APPRAISAL

Let us consider the appraisal of a typical road scheme (Table 5.1). Like any other project, it will involve capital, maintenance and operating costs. Unlike many other projects, the bulk of the operating costs will be incurred by people other than the agency undertaking the project – namely motorists, bus companies and road hauliers. Moreover, to the extent that in the absence of the scheme they would have used poorer quality, more congested roads, operating cost savings appear as a benefit of the scheme; it is only in respect of any traffic generated by the road itself that they appear as a cost. In common with normal Department of Transport practice, the example in Table 5.1 assumes that the scheme itself generates no additional traffic that

Table 5.1 Costs and benefits of a road scheme (present values, £000, in 1979 prices, discounted at 7%)

	Traffic growth (alternative assumptions)	
	High	Low
Costs		
Construction	2 491	2 491
Maintenance	72	72
Delays during construction	32	32
Total	2 595	2 595
Benefits		
Time and operating cost savings	4 218	2 658
Accident savings	417	304
Total	4 635	2 962
Net present value	2 040	367

Source: Institute for Transport Studies, University of Leeds: Economic Evaluation Short Course, course notes.

would not have existed without the scheme, so that operating costs appear solely as a benefit for existing traffic. (This controversial assumption is considered further in section 8.) There may also be some maintenance cost savings on existing roads as a result of the reduced level of traffic using them.

So far, the CBA appears very straightforward. All the above items are readily measured in money terms. However two categories of benefit that are usually much more significant than operating cost savings are time savings and reductions in accidents. Obviously these benefits are not normally traded in any market, therefore we are faced with the problems of imputing values to then.

In the case of time savings, there is a distinction to be made between time spent travelling during working hours (which includes bus and lorry drivers as well as business travellers) and time spent travelling during one's own time. In the former case, it is usual to value the time at the wage rate of the employee concerned plus a mark-up to allow for overhead costs of employing labour (such as social insurance charges). This assumes that the time saved can be gainfully employed and that the gross wage represents the value of the marginal product of labour in its alternative use. Doubts may be raised on a number of grounds. Is the time saving large enough to be of use, or will it simply be wasted as idle time (individual transport projects often yield savings of less than a minute, although these may be aggregated with savings from other schemes to form more useful amounts of time)? Will the labour released find alternative work, or add to unemployment? If it does find alternative employment, does the gross wage really reflect the value of its marginal product in the new use (Marks, Fowkes and Nash, 1986)?

For non-working time, the problem of valuation is greater. The approach here has been to try to discover what people are willing to pay to save time, either by 'revealed preference' or by 'stated preference' methods. Revealed preference methods rely on studying people's behaviour in situations in which they reveal an implicit value of time. The most popular case is that of the choice of travel mode, where people may have a choice between two modes, one of which is faster and more expensive than the other. If a model is estimated which forecasts the probability that someone chooses one mode rather than the other as a function of journey time, money cost and any other relevant quality differences, then the relative weight attached to time and money can be used to estimate their 'value of time'.

This approach was used for many years, but it suffered from some problems. One had to find cases where such trade-offs really exist and are perceived by a representative cross section of the population. To estimate the value of time to a reasonable degree of accuracy, samples running into thousands are needed, and the data usually have to be collected specifically for this purpose by means of a questionnaire survey. If 'stated preference' methods are used, then respondents to the survey are asked what they would choose, given hypothetical alternatives (an example is given in Table 5.2). This enables the individual trade-offs to be designed to reveal the maximum information about the value of time; moreover each respondent can be asked about a number of different choices. This allows great economies in sample size. After piloting and testing to ensure that the results were similar to those produced by revealed preference methods, this approach was used extensively in the studies (MVA Consultants; Institute for Transport Studies, University of Leeds; Transport Studies Unit, University of Oxford, 1987) that determined the values of leisure time currently used in British Department of Transport applications (Table 5.3).

Turning to accidents, the costs may be divided into those that are readily valued in money terms and those that are not. The former include damage to

Table 5.2 *Example of a stated preference question*

Please compare the following alternative combinations of train fare and service level.

A

London, dep.	2.50	3.20	3.50	4.20	4.50
Stockport...	5.10	5.40	6.10	6.40	7.10
Manchester, arr.	5.20	5.50	6.20	6.50	7.20

Fares: one-way £12, return £24
Scheduled journey time: 2hrs 30 mins
Reliability: up to *10* mins late

B

London, dep.	2.50	.	3.50	.	4.50
Stockport...	5.40	.	6.40	.	7.40
Manchester, arr.	5.50	.	6.50	.	7.50

Fares: one-way £10, return £20
Schedule journey time: 3hrs
Reliability: up to *30* mins late

Do you:
definitely prefer A?   probably prefer A?   like A and B equally?   probably prefer B?   definitely prefer B?

Source: Institute for Transport Studies, University of Leeds, questionnaire.

property and vehicles, health service, ambulance and police costs. With slightly more hesitation they may be said to include loss of production due to victims being unable to work (this again is typically valued at the gross wage). What is more difficult is to place a money value on the pain, grief and suffering caused by death or injury in an accident. For many years, in Britain, this value was determined by the political process rather than by the preferences of those directly involved. However it is possible to apply both revealed preference and stated preference techniques to this issue as well. The way to do this is to recognize that transport improvements do not save the lives of specific known individuals; rather they lead to a reduced probability of involvement in an accident for all users. Thus real or hypothetical trade-offs between safety and cost may be used to derive the 'value of a life'. Such a stated preference study (Jones-Lee, 1987) is indeed the basis of the value currently used by the British Department of Transport (Table 5.4),

Table 5.3   Resource values of time per person (pence per hour)

	Average 1986 prices and values
(a) Working time	
Car driver	757.6
Car passenger	605.8
Bus passenger	502.8
Rail passenger	811.4
Underground passenger	737.0
Bus driver	510.0
Bus conductor	498.6
Light goods vehicle occupant	476.1
Other goods vehicle occupant	552.8
All workers	724.8
(b) Non-working time in vehicle	
Standard appraisal value	161.2
People of working age	190.0
Retired people	127.4
All adults	185.0
Children (under 16)	47.6
(c) Walking, waiting and cycling	
Double the in-vehicle values	

Source: Department of Transport, COBA 9 Manual, May 1987.

although there may be doubts as to how well people are able to respond to questions involving changes in very small probabilities.

The British Department of Transport utilizes a computer program (COBA) to calculate the net present value of its trunk road projects. This programme includes the money values of all the items so far discussed, as indeed do the methods used in all the major countries of Western Europe. But it does not value any of the other effects of road schemes, of which by far the most important and controversial are the environmental effects of such schemes. The way in which these 'intangible' effects of transport projects are typically handled is treated in section 4, but first we discuss another controversial issue in transport appraisal – the problem of forecasting traffic levels and consequently the levels of all the above benefits in physical terms.

Table 5.4 Average cost per casualty, by severity (£1985 prices)

	Pre-revision	Post-1987 revision	Post-1988 revision
Fatal	180 330	252 500	500 000*
Serious	8 280	13 500	13 500
Slight	200	280	280

* 1987 prices.
Source: Department of Transport, Valuation of Road Accidents (1988).

3 FORECASTING

It will be clear from the above discussion that forecasting the volume of traffic that will use a proposed transport facility is a key input into the appraisal process. Given that transport projects frequently take ten years to plan, design and build, and are extremely long-lived, it is necessary to forecast a long way into the future. Road projects in Britain are usually appraised over a 30-year life, which requires forecasting for 40 years from the date on which the planning starts. The benefits from a scheme usually rise more than proportionately with the traffic volume, as increased volume leads to worse congestion. Thus the forecast rate of increase in traffic is very important, as well as being subject to great uncertainty. Possible approaches to forecasting range from simple time series models based on aggregate growth in population, incomes and petrol prices to more detailed modelling of trips by purpose and destination (Kanafani, 1983). The approach used by the British Department of Transport combines a car ownership model (based on incomes and driving licence holding) and a car use model (in which the kilometres run per car vary in accordance with incomes and petrol prices). For freight traffic, tonne kilometres are assumed to be proportional to gross domestic product, whilst bus and coach traffic, is assumed constant over time. High and low forecasts are produced on the basis of alternative assumptions about petrol prices and economic growth (Department of Transport, 1989).

Given a traffic forecast, it is necessary to estimate the resulting travel times. The interaction between traffic volumes and speeds is usually estimated by the use of speed–flow relationships, which vary according to the characteristics of the road (lane width, number of lanes and so on). In urban areas, queuing at junctions is a much greater cause of delay, and relationships between delay at junctions and traffic volumes play a more important role.

Regarding accidents, it is usual simply to use a rate per vehicle kilometre for each type of road. Thus, when traffic is diverted from a single carriageway to a dual carriageway or a motorway, a reduction in accidents is forecast simply because the new road is of a type which has a lower accident rate per vehicle kilometre.

4 ENVIRONMENTAL EFFECTS

Road schemes have many important environmental effects, both at local and global level. At the local level, they lead to property demolition, noise nuisance, visual intrusion and air pollution. At the same time, by taking traffic off other, perhaps more environmentally sensitive roads, projects may offer environmental benefits. More globally, road schemes require inputs, such as limestone; to the extent that they generate additional traffic they also require oil production and produce pollutants with more than purely local effects, such as nitrogen oxides (implicated in acid rain) and carbon dioxide (a greenhouse gas).

It is conceivable that ways could be found to value all of these items in money terms. For instance, the effects of property demolition could be studied by means of a contingent valuation survey, asking people the minimum compensation they would need to willingly sell their existing house (this was undertaken as part of the studies of the proposed third London airport in the early 1970s (Dasgupta and Pearce, 1972, ch. 9). Noise, visual amenity and local air pollution have all been valued by means of studies of house price differentials, which are one way in which people indirectly reveal their willingness to pay for a superior environmental quality (Pearce and Markandya, 1989). It has also been suggested that these factors could be amenable to 'stated preference' surveys, perhaps also using house prices as the payment instrument (Nash, 1990).

For global pollutants there is greater difficulty in valuation. Much of this springs from enormous uncertainty as to the physical causation and effects. For instance, what contribution does an extra tonne of nitrogen oxides make to the incidence of acid rain, and what damage does that rain do to plants, wildlife and buildings? Valuing the social cost of carbon dioxide emissions appears even more complex, although attempts have been made to do it. Two such attempts are cited by Pearce (1990).

In the current British methodology, no attempt is made to value environmental effects of road schemes. Rather the environmental effects are set out in a matrix known as the Leitch framework, after the chairman of the committee which devised it (Leitch, 1978). A summary of the elements included in this matrix is shown in Table 5.5. From this it will be seen that there is a wide variety of measures, all in different units – physical measures, numbers of houses, rankings, verbal descriptions. At the same time, no measures are included of non-local environmental effects of schemes. This is because, with traffic assumed constant regardless of what road schemes are built, the level of these pollutants hardly varies.

By contrast, a number of other countries, including Germany and Sweden, do explicitly value certain local environmental effects in their appraisal of transport projects. For instance both of these countries value noise and local air pollution. It must be said, however, that the values used are based on somewhat shaky evidence, and are derived from estimates of the alternative costs of achieving environmental standards by alternative means (such as double glazing, or fitting catalytic convertors to vehicles). This approach presupposes that the standard is appropriate in the first place.

In the British approach, no formal method is used for trading off these various measures against each other and against the 'economic' costs and benefits. At the local level, the Leitch framework is used to reach a judgement as to which of a number of local variants of the scheme is the best overall. Even here there is a suspicion in many quarters that those elements counted as 'economic', which include leisure time savings, are given more weight than those that are not. But it is in setting national priorities between schemes for funding that this suspicion is strongest. How could one possibly use the Leitch framework approach to rank schemes on a national level, for instance to set priorities between bypasses, motorway upgrading, new urban roads and development roads in remote areas? It appears that, to the extent that such comparisons are made at all, they are made largely on the basis of the net present value. This belief is fuelled by the frequency with which figures on the overall returns from the trunk road programme are quoted,

Table 5.5 Costs and benefits of road schemes: the Leitch framework

Incidence group	Nature of effect	Financial	Other units
Road users	Accidents	1	3
	Comfort/convenience	6	
	Operating costs	5	
	Amenity		2
Non-road users directly affected	Demolition disamenity (houses, shops, office, factories schools, churches public open space)		37
	Land take, severance, disamenity to farmers		7
Those concerned	Landscape, scientific, historical value, land use, other transport operators		9 (+ verbal description)
Financing authority	Costs and benefits in money terms	7	
Total		19	59

Source: Leitch (1978).

even though these exclude all environmental effects, as well as being misleading in other respects (see section 6).

Again one may contrast this with the position in most European countries, where the economic costs and benefits are included in what is more obviously a multicriterion framework used for ranking schemes and setting priorities. However it is rare for formal multicriterion techniques to be used in doing this, the principal exception being the Netherlands, where a microcomputer-based decision support system is used.

5 LAND USE AND DEVELOPMENT EFFECTS

In many countries, a main motivation behind transport projects is the encouragement of economic development and the promotion of particular patterns of land use. Thus, for instance, better roads to remote areas may be built to reduce their disadvantage in terms of transport cost; improved public transport to a city centre may be used to try to reduce decentralization of jobs. It is clear from the foregoing that the approach in Britain has generally been to concentrate on the direct transport benefits of projects, on the assumption that these are overwhelmingly the most important factors. Part of the reason for this is that, in a small country with an already well developed transport system, even a major transport project will only have a small effect on the total costs of production and distribution of most industries in a particular location. Typically, in Britain, transport costs amount to some 8 per cent of total production and distribution costs, and even major projects will change total cost by less than 1 per cent (Dodgson, 1973). Moreover, even if one can reduce the disadvantage of remote areas, they will still not be favoured unless they have some advantages which outweigh the fact that their transport costs will still be higher than those in more accessible locations.

Nevertheless there clearly are cases where transport improvements do affect land use and economic development. A major estuary crossing, for example, may enable firms to concentrate their distribution facilities (or even production) on one side of the estuary, with consequent exploitation of economies of scale (Mackie and Simon, 1986). A major motorway development close to a major conurbation will tend to attract distribution and retailing activities, particularly at junctions with other motorways (McKinnon, 1988). Improved rail services to the city centre may well trigger house building for commuter purchase (Harman, 1980). It should be noted that these developments are not always beneficial. In the case of the M25 motorway around London, much new development has been attracted to a green belt area, at considerable environmental cost. Improved roads to remote parts of Scotland may promote tourist travel, but they also enable firms to serve those areas from major centres, leading to the closure of local facilities such as bakers and distribution depots. Improved rail services may lead to the growth of long distance commuting and urban sprawl.

Whilst models do exist to try to predict these sorts of repercussions of transport projects, they are complex to use and they are not yet at the stage that they can be relied on to give more then general guidance on likely effects (Webster, Bly and Paulley, 1988). Thus weighing up of these factors still has to be mainly a matter of judgement. Nevertheless it appears that many European countries pay more attention to regional and land use factors when reaching a view on the overall desirability of a scheme than does Britain.

6 INCOME DISTRIBUTION

It is a common concern that CBA does not take into account the distribution of the benefits and costs of the project concerned. Moreover, by valuing benefits at what people are willing to pay for them, and costs at the compensation people require, it is systematically biased towards the better off, who, other things being equal, will be willing to pay more, and require more compensation. In other words, cost–benefit analysis places more weight on people's preferences the better off they are (Nash, Pearce and Stanley, 1975).

If this aspect of CBA is not liked, then it is necessary to allow decision makers to place more weight on costs and benefits incurred by poorer groups, either by some explicit weighting system, or by providing the information in such a way that they can reach a judgement on this issue too. In other words, costs and benefits need to be presented by incidence group, and information is needed on the incomes of those groups.

The Leitch framework goes some way towards doing this, by dividing costs and benefits into those falling on road users, occupiers of property, those interested in the historical or scientific value of the site and so on. But there are some strange inconsistencies surrounding the treatment of public authorities. There is no clear separation of the cash flow to and from public authorities from the benefits to users – for some reason, both are treated as benefits to the financing authority. This certainly reinforces the view that the financing authority is interested in time savings for users but not in environmental costs and benefits. Amongst other groups for whom benefits are not clearly isolated are companies (involved in freight and business travel), public transport operators, cyclists and pedestrians.

A more consistent approach to the specification and measurement of effects on incidence groups has been developed by Lichfield, initially as the Planning Balance Sheet (Lichfield, Kettle and Whitbread, 1975) and later extended and renamed to form Community Impact Evaluation (Lichfield, 1988). This approach clearly specifies all the relevant groups and consistently identifies costs and benefits to them, either in whatever the natural units of measurement of the effect in question are, or in money units where valuations are deemed to be sufficiently reliable to be of value (Table 5.6). Transfer payments are explicitly included (in contrast to a conventional CBA where they are excluded), but of course they are included both on the cost side and on the benefit side. Thus, for instance, a tax payment appears as a cost to the group of road users paying it and as a benefit to the public authority receiving it.

Two final points may be made on the distributional issue. Firstly, when evaluating methods of valuing time and accident savings, there is – not surprisingly – clear evidence that these are related to ability to pay. Thus, if one were CBA purely as an efficiency test, one would need to disaggregate benefits by income group and apply higher values of these benefits to the better off. This would systematically bias decisions towards improving roads used more by the affluent, for instance those in wealthier parts of the country.

Table 5.6   Brigg Inner Relief Road, impact groups

PRODUCERS
On site
Landowners and occupiers displaced
County Council as Highway Authority
Borough Council as Highway Authority

Off site
Landowners and occupiers not displaced
Landowners – developable sites
Borough Council as authority levying local taxation
Brigg as economic entity
Regional cultural heritage

CONSUMERS
Occupiers of buildings displaced
Vehicular traffic
Occupiers of buildings not displaced
New occupiers in developable sites
Brigg local taxpayers
Brigg residents and visitors

Source: Lichfield (1987).

In practice this has never been seen as politically acceptable. Thus it is usual simply to apply average values to all road users. This in itself could introduce some curious biases to decisions, however. For instance, it may lead authorities to spend money on securing time savings for travellers in poor areas on the basis of the average value of time, when in fact those travellers value the time savings at less than the cost of the scheme, and would rather have received the cash as a tax reduction. This illustrates the problem that effectively uprating *one* item of benefit for the poor whilst not applying similar weights to all others distorts their relative values of different types of cost and benefit. It is more consistent to value all costs and benefits at people's own willingness to pay or to accept compensation, and then to weight the sum total of costs and benefits.

A second and massive problem with distributional analysis arises regarding the incidence of the benefits. It is in the nature of the market system that the final incidence of costs and benefits tends to differ from the initial one. Thus, for instance, environmental and accessibility benefits tend to become capitalized into property values, and thus ultimately to benefit property owners rather than occupiers. Where property is rented rather than owned outright this obviously changes the final incidence of benefits. Similarly benefits to firms may well be passed on through the market. For instance, given the highly competitive nature of both the road haulage and the retail industries, one might reasonably assume that benefits to road hauliers are passed on to retailers in the form of lower freight charges, and ultimately to consumers in the form of lower prices. A reasonable assumption therefore would be that these effects should be shown as benefits to consumers, in proportion to their levels of consumption, rather than to firms.

When these factors are taken into account, a full analysis of the distributional effects of schemes is very much more complex than appears at first sight. It is far easier to undertake an efficiency analysis in which transfers – and therefore redistribution of costs and benefits – are ignored.

7 COMPARABILITY BETWEEN MODES

So far our discussion has focused on road projects as the typical transport application of CBA. However the technique can be readily applied to rail infrastructure projects, air and seaports, and so on. It can also be used to appraise pricing policies and levels of service on public transport. When applied to public transport, broadly the same list of issues arises as considered above in the case of roads. However it should be noted that, given the absence of appropriate pricing to cover the external costs of congestion, accidents and environmental effects on roads, benefits often arise from public transport projects in terms of relieving these problems by diverting traffic from car or lorry.

There is one major difference. In the case of public transport, usually a fare is charged for the journey, and often the fares and service decisions are left to the operator, acting on a commercial basis. This is only possible in the case of road schemes if a toll is charged and this is the exception rather than the rule. Whilst a number of countries (France, Italy and Spain) do have tolls on motorways, this is not yet the case in Britain, with the exception of estuarial crossings. Urban road pricing schemes, although under consideration in the Netherlands, Sweden and Britain, have yet to be implemented anywhere in Europe, with the exception of tolls for crossing the cordons surrounding a number of Norwegian cities. Thus it can usually be assumed that, with the exception of marginal payments of fuel tax, road use is free at the point of use.

At one level, all the presence of commercial public transport operators does is to add a further complication to the analysis. If, for instance, one was examining provision of a facility such as a bus priority system, and the agency undertaking the project had no control over the service decisions of the bus operator, it would simply be necessary to predict the reactions of the operator, just as one needs to predict the behaviour of road users in any road scheme.

However, the question arises as to whether it is desirable to change that behaviour, either by provision of grants or subsidies or by direct ownership and control. Consider, for instance, the case of a rail project, where the rail operator is usually an integrated provider of track and services. If the operator is simply set commercial objectives, it will obviously appraise investment in rail infrastructure solely on financial terms. Many of the items included in the above appraisal – user benefits (except inasmuch as they may be recouped as fare revenue), benefits of relief of road congestion, accidents and environmental degradation, and other environmental effects – will be left out of the appraisal.

Thus the use of CBA for public transport projects inevitably involves some sort of replacement of purely financial objectives with social ones, and usually some sort of grant or subsidy. For governments which believe in leaving decisions to the market wherever possible, perhaps because of a belief that grants or subsidies automatically lead to inefficiency, this is an unwelcome message. This has been the case in Britain in recent times. It has been asserted that in most cases CBA and financial appraisal yield broadly the same conclusions for public transport projects, and thus that one can directly compare cost–benefit rates of return on road schemes and financial rates of return on public transport schemes. The evidence for this assertion comes from a study of a rail project which is reproduced in Table 5.7 (Department of Transport, 1984). It is seen that, in the case of this project, which is an electrification project, the bulk of the benefits take the form of cost reductions, which do indeed figure in both financial and cost–benefit rates of return. However, to the extent that the scheme leads to a service improvement, the extra revenue earned by the rail operator only recoups a small part of the total benefits of the improvement to rail users and remaining road users.

Cost–Benefit Analysis of Transport Projects

Where it is accepted that public transport improvements yield social benefits (for instance in urban areas) grants towards their costs are still available. However, for the purpose of the grant, benefits to users of the system are disallowed; only benefits to third parties are included. This may drastically reduce the allowable benefits of the scheme (Nash and Preston, 1991) and lead to projects failing to go ahead when they are beneficial in straight social cost–benefit terms (see Table 5.8 for an example).

Table 5.7 Birmingham–London/Basingstoke electrification (NPV £ m in 1979 prices at 7%)

Low-growth scenario		
Increase in passenger revenue	+	6 490
Reduction in operating costs	+	27 955
Reduction in capital and maintenance costs	–	40 095
Financial NPV	–	5 650
Consumer surplus to rail users (existing and new)	+	2 857
Consumer surplus to remaining road users	+	1 485
Saving in road accident costs	+	0 440
Tax adjustment	–	1 243
Change in London Transport revenue	–	0 063
Social NPV	–	2 175

Notes:
1. This appraisal covered inter-city passenger services only. Local and suburban services were assumed to remain diesel-operated.
2. Consumer surplus to remaining road users is shown as 1845 in the original, but comparison with figures elsewhere in the report makes it clear that this is an error.

Source: Department of Transport (1984).

It should be stressed that this particular approach to public transport is a peculiarly British one; most European countries routinely conduct cost–benefit analyses of public transport investments and allow grant aid to public transport on the basis of the total benefits it produces. But it does illustrate a more general problem, which is that of reconciling social and commercial aims in the transport sector. It is common for certain forms of publicly provided transport service long-distance rail and bus services; rail freight

Table 5.8 Comparison of net present values of two rail investment programmes (30-year project life, 7% interest rate, £000s, 1986 prices)

	West Yorkshire, 6 new stations on existing services	Leicester–Burton, new service serving 14 new stations
Gain in public transport revenue from new users	99	8 897
Loss in public transport revenue due to increased journey time	−166	—
Recurrent costs	−147	−9 154
Capital costs	−656	−5 806
Financial NPV	28	−6 063
Time savings to new rail users	515	4 582
Time savings to existing rail users	−472	—
Time savings to road users	113	3 304
Accident savings	277	2 612
Tax adjustment	−282	−2 326
Social NPV	179	2 109
Social NPV excluding user benefits	136	−2 473

Source: Nash and Preston (1991).

services) to be provided on a purely commercial basis, but this gives immediate rise to a comparability problem, since a commercial operator will automatically take decisions on a financial rather than a cost–benefit basis. Sometimes it is argued that the solution is to provide the road system on a commercial basis, in the form of toll roads as well. However comparability has little value if it consists of following the wrong criteria on all modes. To the extent that transport is a sector in which externality problems abound, it seems appropriate to use CBA throughout the sector. Provided that grants are only given to public transport operators for specific purposes, and that their use is strictly monitored, any resulting problems of loss of incentives to operate efficiently can be minimized.

8 STRATEGIC CONSIDERATIONS AND THE CONTEXT OF APPRAISAL

Transport projects are typically not free-standing investments but are part of a network. As such there may be strong interdependencies both between investment projects and between investment and other policies such as traffic restraint, pricing changes, land use changes and so on. This greatly complicates the task of the appraiser. It becomes necessary to consider individual projects by themselves, given an assumed strategy and assumptions as to what other projects will be implemented and groups of projects, given an overall strategy and strategies as a whole. Three British examples will be used to demonstrate this point.

The first is again trunk road appraisal in Great Britain. The techniques described above are typically applied to small stretches of trunk road, assuming that a given level of traffic growth will be accommodated (currently 83–142 per cent by 2025) and that other proposed schemes to accommodate this growth will go ahead. Now this is a necessary tactical exercise to appraise the contribution of the particular stretch of road to the overall strategy. But discovering whether accommodating a doubling of traffic is best achieved on the existing road or on a new road is a very weak test of the investment. It is necessary to look at groups of road projects together where, for instance, they upgrade a particular route as a whole, so that the traffic on one section of road is dependent on the other investments going ahead. It is also necessary to look at alternative strategies such as traffic restraint, increased petrol prices and improved public transport, which may together alter the rate of growth of traffic. In any event, even if one individual scheme has little effect on traffic growth (and this is disputed – for instance see Beardwood and Elliot, 1985) it is surely the case that the overall level of investment does affect traffic growth. For instance, it is already observed that traffic growth is very slow in the most congested areas where there is little spare capacity, and surely this phenomenon would spread in the absence of major investment.

It is therefore quite misleading to aggregate returns on individual small schemes and regard this as the rate of return on the roads programme as a whole. Strategic studies are required to show what is the value of alternative aggregate levels of road building in the light of strategic policy alternatives involving different rates of traffic growth.

The second example relates to cities such as London. Both road and rail transport in London are extremely congested and one way of relieving the congestion is to build new underground railways across the centre, at enormous cost (Department of Transport/British Railways Board/London Regional Transport, 1989). One might appraise these projects on the basis of existing policies, in which there is continuing severe congestion on the road. But suppose a different package of policies were to be implemented, involving, for instance, charging a supplementary fee for bringing a car into Central London or other methods of traffic restraint. This might directly increase the demand for rail travel still further. At the same time, it could free buses from road congestion and enable them to play a much more effective part in short-distance public transport. Whether the net effect is to improve or to worsen the case for the new rail tunnels is not clear, but it could hardly be expected to leave it unchanged. In congested urban areas, where modes of transport are particularly strongly interdependent, the need to see investment appraisal as part of an integrated transport planning process is particularly strong.

The third example is internal to the rail system. Rail transport, even more than road, forms a closely integrated network where infrastructure, rolling stock type and the services to be run are particularly closely linked. The case for reconstructing a particular junction or stretch of route to a certain capacity depends on the volume of traffic of each type expected to pass through or over it. That in turn depends on pricing, service level and rolling stock investment plans for all those services, which may include express passenger, local passenger and freight. Similarly it is pointless to resignal a route to allow for higher speeds unless investment is simultaneously made in track and rolling stock to permit those speeds, or to plan for freight wagons and locomotives with heavier axle loads without upgrading track and structures to take them. Since rolling stock may be switched from one part of the system to another as part of an investment strategy, railway appraisals often need to look far and wide, and may need to consider the network as a whole. (See, for instance, the financial appraisals of the case for main line railway electrification published in Department of Transport/British Railways Board, 1981).

The point of this section is to stress, then, that in all modes of transport there is a need to look not just at individual projects but also at alternative packages of projects and at projects as a whole in the light of feasible alternative strategies. This has been the practice in a number of recent British urban transport studies, such as those in Birmingham and Edinburgh (May, 1991). But again this is an area where many continental countries appear to have organized themselves better than Britain. Several countries (such as Germany and Sweden) explicitly consider the allocation of national transport infrastructure funds across all modes as part of a coordinated programme using comparable investment criteria. The Netherlands has gone a stage further in seeking to make this procedure part of an overall plan to influence transport demand and supply to achieve specific accessibility and environmental targets. Whilst the various elements of the plan may not be as internally consistent as appears at first sight, this represents one of the few attempts to relate project appraisal to strategic plans at the national level within Europe.

9 ALTERNATIVE APPROACHES TO APPRAISAL

So far, the examples of transport appraisals used in this chapter have been based largely on methods devised by the British Department of Transport for central government use. Local authorities have tended to take a somewhat different approach. Perhaps because they are more concerned with planning and environmental issues than with narrow transport benefits, they have been much more ready to adopt objectives achievement or other multicriteria appraisal methods. We have also already commented on the fact that appraisals in many other European countries are more explicitly multicriteria in orientation, with economic efficiency seen as one of a number of objectives.

Multicriteria approaches are considered in detail in Chapter 3 and this section will confine itself to some comments on how they are typically used in the transport sector. These approaches require three stages: firstly, definition of a set of objectives, which may for instance relate to accessibility, the environment, safety, economy and equity; next, measurement of the extent to which each project contributes towards the desired objective; finally, weighting of the measures in order to aggregate them and produce a ranking of projects (Mackie *et al.*, 1990).

As it stands, this method would be quite consistent with the principles of cost–benefit analysis if the following conditions held: (1) all the objectives related to factors that affect the welfare of the population concerned, and (2) the measures of achievement and weighting of them are based on the preferences of the people affected by the projects, subject possibly to some form of equity weighting. In practice, the first condition probably generally holds but the second does not. Measurement of the degree of contribution to objectives is often based not on detailed measurement but on the judgement of the professional staff planning the projects. This may be defensible where the schemes are small enough to make detailed study too costly, but otherwise it is not. Relative weighting of the measures of achievement is likewise usually based on the value judgement of the decision taker rather than the preferences of the people directly affected by the scheme. All too often, too, these relative weights are obtained with too little consideration of the differing units of measurement of the performance measures regarding the different objectives.

Whether these weightings are expressed in money terms or not, they are essentially performing the same function as money values in expressing relative valuations. Moreover, to the extent that at least one of the performance measures − cost or economy − is expressed in money terms, they can readily be transformed into money values. There is therefore less difference between this approach and traditional CBA than might at first sight be supposed.

What clearly is a major difference is the use of decision takers' preferences. Now it is clear that a CBA rests on certain value judgements; namely that decisions should be based on the preferences of those affected by the projects, and that these preferences should be weighted in a certain way (according to income if unweighted willingness to pay type measures are used). If the decision taker for some reason rejects those value judgements, he or she will clearly wish to impose their own preferences or weights. Nor would the present author wish to deny the right of the decision taker to do this, as long as they are in some way democratically accountable for their actions.

It appears then that, as currently practised, multicriteria decision-making techniques are essentially concerned with aiding and ensuring consistency in this latter stage of weighting by the decision taker. This is a separate role from that played by the CBA, and should be seen as complementary rather than competing. To the extent that the information provided by a CBA is seen as relevant to the decision taker, it still needs to be provided. But what is clear is that it must be provided in a sufficiently disaggregated form for the decision taker to apply, explicitly or implicitly, his or her own weights. This again argues for the Planning Balance Sheet or Community Impact Evaluation form of presentation as outlined briefly in section 6 above.

10 CONCLUSION

We have found many criticisms of the application of CBA to transport projects as generally practised. Foremost amongst the perceived faults are the failure to conduct appraisals at a strategic level, so that a full range of options is not properly considered, and a failure to look beyond the direct effects (construction, maintenance and operating costs, time and accident savings) to quantify and value a full range of relevant effects. Whilst examples can be found of countries where current practice is ahead of that in Britain (for example the role of strategic planning in the Netherlands and the efforts to quantify environmental costs in money terms in Germany and Sweden), in no cases can it be said that the treatment of these crucial issues is wholly satisfactory.

This sounds a fairly damning indictment of CBA as it is currently used, but it is important to realize that a simple switch to an alternative approach, based on objectives satisfaction or multicriteria methods, will not of itself solve this problem. Indeed, inasmuch as the current approach inevitably ends up with a list of effects which cannot be valued in money terms, it is already, at least in an informal sense, a multicriteria approach. What we would advocate is that a thorough attempt should always be made to identify all relevant effects of projects and to trace these back to appropriate incidence groups. For this purpose, we strongly commend the Planning Balance Sheet or Community Impact Evaluation approach. At this stage, where reliable monetary valuations of externalities can be shown they provide useful information on the preferences of those affected regarding how much it is worth spending to secure those particular benefits or to remove those particular costs.

The final task of the decision taker is to weigh up these costs and benefits one with another, taking account of who gains and who loses. Where repeated similar decisions have to be made it may be worth using some formal weighting system at this stage, and computerized systems which enable the decision taker to explore the sensitivity of decisions to the weights used have great value. Thus a sensible approach will almost certainly combine elements of CBA and multicriteria decision-taking systems. It is as foolish to consider that decisions can be reduced to the simple calculation of a net present value as to believe that monetary valuation has no role in decision taking.

BIBLIOGRAPHY

Beardwood, J. and Elliot, J. (1985), 'Roads Generate Traffic', Planning and Transportation Research and Computation Summer Annual Meeting, University of Sussex.

Beesley, M.E. and Foster, C.D. (1963), 'Estimating the social benefits of constructing an underground railway in London', *Journal of the Royal Statistical Society*, Series A, **126**, (1).

Beesley, M.E., Coburn, T.M. and Reynolds, D.J. (1960), *The London–Birmingham Motorway – Traffic and Economics*, Road Research Laboratory Technical Paper 46, Crowthorne, Berks.

Dasgupta, A.K. and Pearce, D.W. (1972), *Cost Benefit Analysis: Theory and Practice*, London: Macmillan.

Department of Transport (1984), *Economic Evaluation Comparability Study – Final Report*, London: Department of Transport.

Department of Transport (1989), *National Road Traffic Forecasts*, London: Department of Transport.

Department of Transport/British Railways Board (1981), *Review of Main Line Electrification. Final Report*, London: HMSO.

Department of Transport/British Railways Board/London Regional Transport (1989), *Central London Rail Study*, London: Department of Transport.

Dodgson, J.S. (1973), 'External Effects in Road Investment', *Journal of Transport Economics and Policy*, 7.

Harman, R. (1980), *Great Northern Electrics in Hertfordshire*, Hertford: Hertfordshire County Council.

Jones-Lee, M. (1987), 'The Value of Transport Safety', *Policy Journals*, Newbury, Berks.

Kanafani, A. (1983), *Transportation Demand Analysis*, New York: McGraw-Hill.

Leitch, Sir George, Chairman (1978), *Report of the Advisory Committee on Trunk Road Appraisal*, London: HMSO.

Lichfield, N. (1987), 'Brigg Economic Regeneration Study: Evaluation of Inner Relief Road', unpublished report, Nathaniel Lichfield and Partners Ltd., London.

Lichfield, N. (1988), *Economics in Urban Conservation*, Cambridge: Cambridge University Press.

Lichfield, N., Kettle, P. and Whitbread, M. (1975), *Evaluation in the Planning Process*, Oxford: Pergamon Press.

Mackie, P.J. and Simon, D. (1986), 'Do Road Projects Benefit Industry? A Case Study of the Humber Bridge', *Journal of Transport Economics and Policy*, **20**, (3).

Mackie, P.J., May, A.D., Pearman, A.D. and Simon, D. (1990), *Computer-Aided Assessment for Transportation Policies*, New York: Greenwood Press.

Marks, P., Fowkes, A.S. and Nash, C.A. (1986), 'Valuing Long Distance Business Travel Time Savings for Evaluation; A Methodological Review and Application', Planning and Transportation Research and Computation Summer Annual Meeting, Seminar on Transportation Planning Methods, University of Sussex.

May, A.D. (1991), 'Integrated transport strategies: a new approach to urban transport policy in the U.K.', *Transport Reviews*, **11**, (3), pp. 223–47.

McKinnon, A.C. (1988), 'Recent Trends in Warehouse Location', in Cooper, James (ed.), *Logistics and Distribution Planning. Strategies for Management*, London: Kogan Page.

MVA Consultants; Institute for Transport Studies, University of Leeds; Transport Studies Unit, University of Oxford (1987), 'The Value of Travel Time Savings'. *Policy Journals*, Newbury, Berks.

Nash, C.A., (ed.) (1990), *Appraising the Environmental Effects of Road Schemes: A Response to the Standing Advisory Committee on Trunk Road Assessment*, Institute for Transport Studies Working Paper 293, University Of Leeds.

Nash, C.A., and Preston, J. (1991), 'Appraisal of Rail Investment Projects: Recent British Experience', *Transport Reviews*, **11**, (4).

Nash, C.A., Pearce, D.W. and Stanley, J.K. (1975), 'An Evaluation of Cost–Benefit Analysis Criteria', *Scottish Journal of Political Economy*, June.

Pearce, D.W. (1990), 'The Valuation of Transport-Induced Environmental Costs and Benefits', paper presented at the Seminar on Longer Term Issues, Department of Transport, London.

Pearce, D.W. and Markandya, A. (1989), *Environmental Policy Benefits: Monetary Valuation*, Paris: OECD.

Sanderson, I. (1989), 'Road Investment Appraisal Techniques in Europe: Some International Comparisons', Institute for Transport Studies, University of Leeds, unpublished.

Webster, F.V., Bly, P.H. and Paulley, N.J. (1988), *Urban Land-use and Transport Interaction. Policies and Models*, Aldershot: Avebury.

6. Cost–Benefit Analysis in Health and Health Care: Fine in Practice, but Does it Work in Theory?

Michael F. Drummond

1 INTRODUCTION

The aim of this chapter is to give an assessment of the current state of the art of cost–benefit analysis (CBA) in health care. The body of work upon which comments are based consists of several surveys of practice (Drummond, 1981a; Warner and Luce, 1982; Drummond *et al.*, 1986; Luce and Elixhauser, 1990) and other papers, written by health economists, in which the conceptual issues surrounding the use of CBA are discussed. The starting-point will be the 'traditional' welfare economics notion that the purpose of CBA is to identify potential Pareto improvements; that is, situations where the maximum total sum of money that the gainers from a project or programme would be prepared to pay to ensure that the project was undertaken exceeds the minimum total sum of money that the losers from it would accept as compensation to allow it to be undertaken. However, as will be discussed later, the practice of CBA in health and health care has departed considerably from this theoretical position.

The chapter is organized as follows. First, the special characteristics of health and health care are outlined, since they partly condition the application of CBA in this field. Then attention is turned to the precise formulations of CBA used in the appraisal of alternatives in health and health care. This is followed by more detailed examination of particular aspects of CBA in practice, including the selection of alternatives for appraisal, the assessment of costs and benefits, and the analysis of distributive effects. In conclusion, an overall assessment of the contribution of CBA in this field is made and the remaining methodological concerns are identified.

2 SPECIAL CHARACTERISTICS OF HEALTH AND HEALTH CARE

In the health economics literature, health care is considered to be only one input to the production of health (Grossman, 1972). Indeed other inputs, such as education or other environmental factors, may be just as important as health care in many situations (Fuchs, 1986). Similarly the demand for health care is viewed as a derived demand, the more fundamental demand being that for health itself. Nevertheless the vast majority of the health economics literature considers the economics of health *care* and interest has centred on the special characteristics of health *care* as a commodity. These have been well documented elsewhere (Culyer, 1976) and include the lack of consumer information, the uncertainty in future consumption and the existence of externalities. In some cases health care can be said to exhibit merit good characteristics, as in the case of treatment for mental illness, or public good characteristics, as in the case of some broad public health measures (for example, fluoridation of water supplies).

Economists differ in their beliefs about the extent to which these special characteristics lead to market failure. However there are several features of the provision of health care that have implications for the practice of CBA. First, in almost all developed countries there is extensive government intervention in health care markets. This is taken by many to signify a concern for equity in access to services, which presumably flows from the existence of externalities. Secondly, health care is not a widely traded commodity, which means that there are few observable market prices to give a preliminary basis for the valuation of health care outputs. Thirdly, where health care is traded, the asymmetry of information between the supplier (doctor and other health professional) and the consumer (patient) is likely to lead to market imperfections, the most well documented of which is the potential for supplier-induced demand (Evans, 1974).

3 FORMULATIONS OF CBA IN HEALTH AND HEALTH CARE

The practice of CBA in the health care field exhibits a number of departures from classical CBA, many of which stem from the special characteristics of health care identified above. However, in considering these departures from the traditional welfare economics theory, it is important to note that the Paretian approach is not the only recognized form of CBA. An alternative approach, outlined by Sugden and Williams (1979), starts from the premise that the relevant question to ask is, 'What objective would a social decision-maker choose to pursue?' They suggest that 'there is a strong argument that, at least in a fairly centralized public decision-making system, the objective chosen normally will correspond to that implied by the potential Pareto improvement criterion' if the government, through its control of the tax system, has the power to convert potential Pareto improvements into actual Pareto improvements. Of course a problem arises if, in examining particular projects or programmes, one cannot assume this to be the case. Therefore, in this *decision-making approach* to CBA, it is likely that the analyst would consider other social objectives in addition to efficiency. The analysis becomes more of an interchange between the analyst and the social decision maker, and a forum for making the decision maker's values explicit.

Most CBA in health and health care is closer to the decision-making, rather than the Paretian, tradition. Whether this is by accident or design is less clear. It may be that analysts are questioning the appropriateness of the value judgements underlying the Paretian approach, given the nature of the commodity health care. On the other hand limitations in the methods for valuing the willingness to pay for improved health or health care may have caused analysts to depart from the Paretian approach as a matter of expediency. The most obvious case of this is the use of the human capital approach to value human life or reductions in morbidity. (This is discussed further later.)

A good example of the practice of CBA in health care is found in the study by Weisbrod *et al.* (1980) comparing community-based and institution-oriented treatments for mental illness patients. This considered a wide range of costs, falling on various public agencies, in direct treatment, law enforcement and patient maintenance. It also considered costs borne by the family in lost earnings (see Table 6.1). The benefits considered included the earnings obtained by the patient and several other intangible items that were hard to quantify. Therefore the range of costs and benefits typically considered by CBAs in health care are C_1–C_3 and B_1–B_3 in Figure 6.1.

However Figure 6.1 also outlines two other approaches to the measurement of the outputs of health care programmes, which give rise to other forms of analysis. First, outputs are sometimes measured in the most obvious natural units or health effects. For example, a life-extending treatment might be judged in terms of its cost per life-year gained; a treatment for a disabling health condition might be judged in terms of its cost per disability day avoided. This form of analysis, known as *cost-effectiveness analysis* (CEA), has the advantage that controversial issues of benefit valuation are avoided, but it has the obvious disadvantages that the output measures used are quite restricted and only limited comparisons, among programmes generating benefits of the same type, can be made. Nevertheless the approach can be quite powerful where the treatment objective is not being questioned directly

Table 6.1 Comparative costs of two programmes for mental illness patients (US dollars)

	Conventional hospital-oriented programme	Community-based programme
Direct treatment costs (borne by the main care agency)	3 138	4 798
Indirect treatment costs		
Other hospital care	1 744	646
Sheltered workshops	91	870
Other community agencies (e.g. social services, visiting nurse service)	285	310
Medical practitioners	22	12
Law enforcement costs	409	350
Patient maintenance costs (borne by government agencies)	1 487	1 035
Family burden costs (e.g. lost earnings due to patient)	120	72
Total	7 296	8 093

Source: Weisbrod *et al.* (1980)

and where there is a single, unambiguous objective of therapy, such as in the treatment of end-stage renal failure (Ludbrook, 1981).

In most situations, however, economists *do* wish to question whether or not treatment should be given and wish to inform broader issues of resource allocation. Owing to the measurement difficulties with CBA, a second, new form of analysis, known as *cost-utility analysis* (CUA) (Drummond *et al.*, 1987) has been gaining popularity. Cost-utility analysis is merely a special form of cost-effectiveness analysis, where the outputs of programmes are measured in terms of health status or health 'utilities'. The most common approach is to measure the outputs in terms of the quality-adjusted life-years

Figure 6.1 Components of economic evaluation

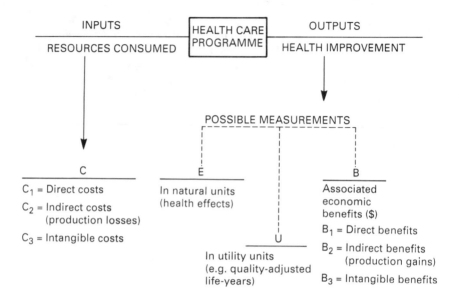

(QALYs) gained (see Figure 6.2). The logic is that health care interventions add either to the length of life or to quality of life. If health-related quality of life can be measured on a scale from zero (dead) to unity (perfect health) an index of QALYs gained can be calculated for different health care interventions. If these outputs are then related to the costs of the respective interventions, the relative value for money from alternative interventions can be assessed (see Table 6.2). Thus cost-utility analysis is accomplishing much that would be achieved by CBA, in that it can inform priorities for resource allocation. It does not, however, tell us what a QALY is worth and therefore defines no threshold value of cost per QALY beyond which a given intervention is not worthwhile. Whether or not this is a serious limitation depends on one's view about the method of determining the size of the health care budget. If, at this level of aggregation, the assignment of budgets between health, education, defence and other public sector activities is essentially a political decision, then the main task for CBA in health care is to ensure that the assigned budget is spent efficiently. If, on the other hand, one takes the view that a key task of CBA is to help determine the allocation of funds to health care, then cost-utility analysis has serious limitations.

Another important aspect of the formulation of CBA in health and health care is in the selection of the *viewpoint* for the analysis. The assumption of

Cost–Benefit Analysis in Health and Health Care   111

Figure 6.2 Quality-adjusted life-years added by treatment

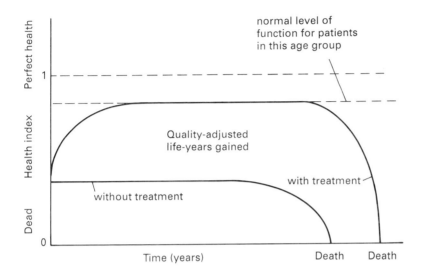

Table 6.2 'League table' of costs and QALYS for selected health care interventions (1983/4 prices)

Intervention	Present value of extra cost per QALY gained (£)
GP advice to stop smoking	170
Pacemaker implantation for heart block	700
Hip replacement	750
CABG for severe angina LMD	1 040
GP control of total serum cholesterol	1 700
CABG for severe angina with 2VD	2 280
Kidney transplantation (cadaver)	3 000
Breast cancer screening	3 500
Heart transplantation	5 000
CABG for mild angina 2VD	12 600
Hospital haemodialysis	14 000

Notes: CABG - coronary artery bypass grafting; LMD - left main disease; 2VD - two vessel disease.
Source: Adapted from Williams (1985).

CBA is that the appropriate viewpoint is that of society. However, whilst most CBAs in health care acknowledge the societal viewpoint, many assess costs and benefits from more restricted viewpoints. A common viewpoint is that of the government, or other 'third party payer', which bears most of the direct costs of the programmes. A smaller number of evaluations take the viewpoint of a particular institution, such as the hospital, but these are more appropriately viewed as financial appraisals. Whether or not the adoption of the government or third party payer viewpoint is broad enough to justify calling a study a CBA is open to question. However it is frequently the case that consideration of a broader range of costs and benefits, such as those falling on patients, their families and society as a whole, would merely serve to reinforce the result obtained by considering the more limited government viewpoint. See, for example, the study by Helliwell and Drummond (1988) on immunizing the elderly against influenza.

In summary it can be seen that CBAs in health and health care often depart from the form implicit in 'classical' CBA. Cost-effectiveness analysis and cost-utility analysis are more common that CBA and frequently the societal perspective is not fully explored. This reflects the practical measurement problems, the nature of the commodity health care and the requirements of the major funders of health care, who are in the main commissioners of studies. In the discussion that follows the term 'CBA' will be used to denote the generic application of the various economic evaluation techniques in health care, whilst recognizing that the specific form of analysis may differ from study to study.

4 ALTERNATIVES ASSESSED BY 'CBA' IN HEALTH AND HEALTH CARE

The first point to note is that most 'CBA' has been of alternatives in health *care*. Appraisal of other health-promoting measures, in education, agricultural policy or road transport, has been relatively neglected. However Jones-Lee's work on the value of human life (Jones-Lee, 1976) was motivated primarily by the need to improve the estimates used in road transport appraisals in the UK. In addition, Graham and Vaupel (1981) have examined the relative cost per life-year gained of different public policy decisions in the USA, in the fields of road safety, environmental protection, health care and occupational health and safety. They found that health care interventions were, on average, relatively cost-effective, especially when compared with those in environmental protection and occupational health. There are also additional benefits accruing from these measures in other fields.

There has also been relatively little investigation of health-promoting measures carried out within the health care sector. In one recent study, Kristiansen et al. (1991) assessed the cost-effectiveness of lowering cholesterol levels in the Norwegian male population through the promotion of healthier eating habits. Cribb and Haycox (1989) argue that it may be difficult to capture the benefits of health promotion programmes by health status measures, such as quality-adjusted life-years gained. They suggest that it may be difficult to establish that such programmes improve health status and that increasing the awareness of individuals about health-related choices constitutes a benefit in its own right, whether or not those individuals subsequently change their health behaviour. Arguing from a theoretical perspective, Cohen and Henderson (1988) point out that there are a number of utility gains from health promotion programmes that bear only indirect relation to improved health status, either now or in the future.

The role of 'CBA' in appraising health care interventions has been much more extensive. For example, a review undertaken for the European Community in 1987 (Drummond, 1987a) found that appraisals had been undertaken in most of the member states, with the greatest number being in Spain, the UK and The Netherlands. The literature in the USA is the most extensive world-wide. A wide range of alternatives has been appraised; these can be classified as follows.

Alternatives in the Prevention of Disease

These would include immunization programmes (Helliwell and Drummond, 1988) and screening programmes (Mugarra and Cabasés, 1990). Essentially the economic question is whether earlier intervention in the course of a disease, by primary or secondary prevention, is justified in terms of its costs and benefits. Another key issue relates to the question of how expensive prevention programmes should be; should they be aimed at high-risk groups or be applied to the whole population?

Alternatives in Diagnosis

These choices mainly relate to the application of new diagnostic technologies, such as CT scanners (Thomson, 1977). These devices are often expensive and the question is whether the benefits of superior diagnostic accuracy justify any additional cost. Since the objective is to improve health, the benefits from a better diagnosis critically depend on the availability of effective treatments. Alternatively a better diagnosis might avert the application of a treatment in error. Other economic issues relate to how extensive the search for an accurate diagnosis should be in situations where effective treatments do not exist (Levine *et al.*, 1985). However, as in the case of health promotion, some argue that the information gains from better diagnosis may be of value in their own right, even if the treatment of the patient is unchanged.

Alternatives in Treatment

This comprises the largest group of appraisals, as might be expected, given the plethora of medical interventions. 'CBAs' have been undertaken of alternative treatments for the same clinical condition, such as drug therapy versus surgery for duodenal ulcer (Culyer and Maynard, 1981). They have also addressed the question of whether it is worthwhile, in terms of relative costs and benefits, to initiate extra treatment, such as adding a second drug to moderate the side-effects of the first (Knill-Jones *et al.*, 1990). In assessing whether any treatment at all is worthwhile, the 'do-nothing' option is usually considered, although it has to be remembered that doing nothing is rarely a costless activity in the health care field since, with end-stage disease in particular, basic ethical principles often dictate that some care be given (Drummond, 1990).

Alternative Settings for Care

These alternatives arise in both the acute and the chronic care fields. For example, an elective surgical procedure may be given on an in-patient or day-case (or out-patient) basis (Russell *et al.*, 1977). In the care of the elderly, patients may be maintained in their own homes through the addition of community services, rather than being institutionalized (Wright *et al.*, 1981). The main contribution of 'CBA' here has been to point out that, in deciding between different settings for care, a wide range of costs needs to be considered. These include not only those falling on the health care agency concerned, but also those falling on other public agencies (such as social services), patients and their families (in providing food, shelter and informal nursing) and the voluntary sector. In general 'CBAs' have been less successful in valuing the relative benefits of care, owing to the measurement difficulties outlined above. It is often assumed that maintaining a person at home is to be preferred. This may usually be the case for the patient, but not necessarily so for the family. A recent cost-utility analysis (Drummond *et al.*, 1991) has considered care giver burden and assessed the cost per QALY gained from a care giver support programme.

Alternative Systems of Health Care Organization

Until recently there had been relatively few 'CBAs' in this category, with the greatest emphasis being on the evaluation of medical procedures. However, in 1981, government directives in the UK led to a growing number of appraisals of hospital building programmes (DHSS, 1981). These appraisals consider the capital and revenue costs of the alternatives, accessibility of hospital sites to patients, visitors and staff, and certain quality measures relating to the physical fabric of buildings, the proximity of essential support services and quality of care (often measured by staffing ratios) (Akehurst, 1989). Rarely are all the benefits expressed in money terms. Rather the appraisals are often used as a vehicle for making explicit the trade-offs necessary in choosing between hospital locations. For example, in order to achieve a higher standard of building quality, access times might be increased since a new hospital site may have to be found away from major centres of population. 'CBAs' in this category are probably closest to the large project appraisals undertaken in other sectors and could be viewed as examples of the multicriteria approach. However, in the main, analysts have opted for explicit weighting schemes for benefits rather like those outlined by Lichfield *et al.* (1977) as an alternative to money valuation, as in 'classical' CBA.

In addition, there have been a few appraisals of alternatives in clinical service delivery. These include assessments of different ways of providing domiciliary oxygen in the UK (Lowson *et al.*, 1981) and alternative locations for epilepsy clinics in Germany (Kreidel, 1980).

The concentration of economic analysts on medical procedures and treatment technologies, rather than large project appraisals, has two strengths and two weaknesses. The first strength is that in the health care sector the major resource allocation decisions flow mainly from choices in treatment technology. Therefore, in concentrating on these choices, it could be argued that 'CBAs' are tackling the key decisions. Secondly, detailed examinations of particular medical options enables the relevant margins to be identified. That is, few medical procedures or technologies are totally worthless. The key questions relate to *how much* they are applied. That is, on which patients should they be applied, and how frequently?

The first weakness of concentrating on individual procedures is that the overview is sometimes lost in the detail. For example, in judging whether a new technology, such as cimetidine therapy for ulcer disease, should be adopted, an examination by 'CBA' of one indication for its use does not give an adequate picture of the technology's overall impact. In a more aggregate study, Bulthuis (1984) assessed the economic impact of the launch of cimetidine in The Netherlands. This impact would include its use in both proven and unproven clinical indications.

The second weakness is that the link between the economic appraisal and the decision is harder to establish. In cases where a major capital investment decision, such as building a road, a power station or hospital, is being made there is a visible decision-making process to which the 'CBA' can be related. In the health care field decisions on the use of individual medical procedures are made by independent medical practitioners. Therefore it is not immediately clear who the client(s) for the results of the 'CBA' are. Should they be the practitioners themselves, or the health service planners who make available the facilities for the clinicians to practise? Thus a distinctive feature of the health care sector is that important resource allocation decisions are being taken at a number of levels in the system: in planning and management, in clinical policy and in individual patient management (Drummond, 1987b). Given this situation, it is understandable that practitioners of 'CBA' have used individual treatments or programmes as the major vehicle for their research.

5 ASSESSMENT OF COSTS AND BENEfiTS

The range of costs and benefits typically considered in an economic appraisal of health care programmes was briefly outlined in Figure 6.1. Figure 6.3 shows the relevant changes in more detail. The first point to note is that the assessment of the benefits of health care interventions is highly dependent on the underlying medical evidence (that is, changes in health state). Therefore there has been a growth in undertaking 'CBAs' alongside clinical trials, which are the main vehicle for assessing medical interventions. There are a number of practical issues in assessing the changes, in resource use or health, in physical terms when comparing two or more medical procedures (Drummond and Davies, 1991). For example, little thought has been given to the appropriate sample size required to detect economically important differences in cost at the conventional levels of statistical significance. However the focus here will be on aspects of the *valuation* of these changes, since this is the main objective of 'CBA' and where practice in the health care field differs most from that in other sectors.

Turning first to costs, it would be fair to say that analysts in the health care field have paid relatively little attention to whether the prices observed reflect true social opportunity costs, or whether shadow prices should be calculated. Indeed most of the examples are in the early literature, such as

Figure 6.3 *The relevant changes in a comparison of the economic efficiency of treatment*

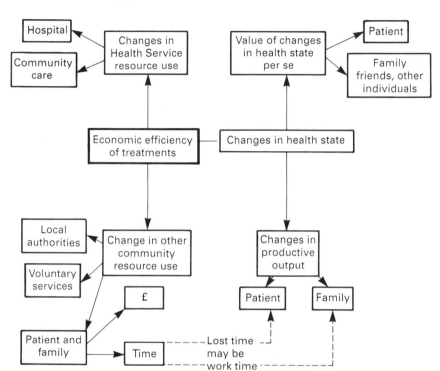

the study by Wager (1972) who deducted the fuel tax from the cost of home nursing. There are also a few examples where analysts have imputed a value for patients' time when the observed price is zero (Schweitzer, 1974). However, overall the only subset of the 'CBA' literature in health care where these issues are taken seriously is in the appraisal of health programmes in developing countries (Mills, 1985).

There are two possible explanations for this lack of concern about the welfare significance of prices. First, if much of the 'CBA' in health care is, indeed, grounded in the decision-making (rather than Paretian) approach, adjustments to prices may be less important if the objective is to initiate an interchange between the analyst and social decision maker, who in many cases will also have the power to influence many health sector prices (for example in agreeing the wage rates of health professionals).

Second, the concentration on the specific viewpoints of particular decision makers (for example, the government), rather than that of society as a whole, suggests that in many cases the relevant prices will be those actually paid.

Even in this context there has been some discussion about whether the charges made by hospitals reflect true costs (Finkler, 1982). However, many 'CBAs' in the health care field are probably closer to being sophisticated financial appraisals than 'classical' cost–benefit analyses.

Turning to the assessment of benefits, it has already been mentioned that the valuation of improvements in health *per se* has posed considerable methodological challenges. The early literature followed the *human capital* approach, where the value of reductions in mortality and morbidity were estimated by using the change in the present value of future earnings to the individuals concerned. Sometimes the estimate was taken net of consumption if the objective was to estimate the value to the rest of the community of maintaining a person's health.

The practice of using the present value of future earnings as a measure of the *total* economic benefits of improved health is now largely discredited and is rarely used. Paradoxically, given what has been said about departures from classical CBA above, one of the main reasons was that the human capital approach is inconsistent with economic theory. Most 'CBA' practitioners in the health care field recognize that it would be better to have a measure based on individuals' willingness to pay for improved health. Also it has been recognized that much health care is delivered to people who are not in paid employment, so there must be major benefits over and above the ability to return to work.

There is more dispute among health economists as to whether discounted future earnings (in so far as they reflect changes in productivity) should be included as *part* of the benefits of health care programmes, or netted out of the numerator (cost) in a cost-effectiveness or cost-utility analysis. Some argue that additions to the workforce at times of near full employment create extra resources and should therefore be considered alongside the other resource changes. Others argue that changes in earnings are a bad measure of changes in productivity and that, in any case, inclusion of these in the analysis will bias health care priorities towards the economically productive and away from groups such as the elderly or mentally handicapped. Also, depending upon how the changes in health *per se* are valued, there may be problems of double counting if productivity changes are also included (Drummond, 1981b).

If the human capital approach has been discredited, what progress has been made with other approaches and are they more closely aligned to economic theory? As mentioned earlier, the major advance has been in the valuation of health states, relative to one another, on a scale from zero to unity. These health state valuations have been referred to in the literature as 'utilities', since one of the methods used to elucidate preferences is the standard gamble developed by von Neumann and Morgenstern (1944). However there is now agreement that the valuations produced do not represent utilities in the classical economics sense (Mehrez and Gafni, 1989; Torrance and Feeny, 1989; Loomes and McKenzie, 1989). Also other methods have been used to elucidate health state valuations, such as the rating scale, the time trade-off and magnitude estimation (Drummond *et al.*, 1987; Kind, Rosser and Williams, 1982).

There are three strands to the health utilities literature. The first approach, epitomized by the work of Stason and Weinstein (1977), does not seek to obtain values directly from individuals. Rather valuations are obtained from experts and the estimates varied to assess whether different assumed values significantly affect the study results. The second approach seeks to develop a generic index which can be applied to all health conditions. The index can then be 'weighted' by obtaining values from individuals for the different index states. Table 6.3 shows the 'Rosser–Kind' index, which defines 32 combinations of disability and distress. The third approach is to obtain direct valuations from individuals of states of health that are relevant to the alternatives being evaluated, for example kidney dialysis (Table 6.4 shows a number of such valuations obtained by Torrance and others in Canada).

Each approach has its advantages and disadvantages, but the common objective is to assess the benefits of health care interventions in terms of the quality-adjusted life-years gained (see Figure 6.2). The use of QALYs, in

Table 6.3   Valuation matrix for 70 respondents

Disability rating		Distress rating		
	A none	B mild	C moderate	D severe
1. No disability	1.000	0.995	0.990	0.967
2. Slight social disability	0.990	0.986	0.973	0.932
3. Severe social disability and/or slight physical impairment	0.980	0.972	0.956	0.912
4. Physical ability severely limited (e.g. light housework only)	0.964	0.956	0.942	0.870
5. Unable to take paid employment or education, largely housebound	0.946	0.935	0.900	0.700
6. Confined to chair or wheelchair	0.875	0.845	0.680	0.000
7. Confined to bed	0.677	0.564	0.000	−1.486
8. Unconscious	−1.078	*	*	*

Notes: Healthy = 1.0; dead = 0.0; * = not applicable.
Source: Kind *et al.* (1982).

particular the calculation of rankings of health care interventions in terms of their cost per QALY, as in Table 6.2, has been the source of heated debate. The approach has been criticized on both practical and theoretical grounds (Mehrez and Gafni, 1989; Loomes and McKenzie, 1989), but it is still the most powerful approach to economic evaluation yet developed by practitioners of 'CBA' in the health care field. In particular it avoids the problems of money valuation, yet deals with the fact that health care interventions have differing impacts on length and quality of life. It generates an explicit set of weights which can then be debated by the decision maker and represents an improvement on the current methods by which health care priorities

Table 6.4 *Mean daily health state 'utilities' in the general population sample*

Duration	Health state	Observations Total	Usable	Mean daily health state utility	Standard error
	Reference state: perfect health			1.00	
3 months	home confinement for tuberculosis	246	239	0.68	0.020
3 months	home confinement for an unnamed contagious disease	246	240	0.65	0.022
3 months	hospital dialysis	246	243	0.62	0.023
3 months	hospital confinement for tuberculosis	246	241	0.60	0.022
3 months	hospital confinement for an unnamed contagious disease	246	242	0.56	0.023
3 months	depression	246	243	0.44	0.024
8 years	home dialysis	246	240	0.65	0.018
8 years	mastectomy for injury	60	56	0.63	0.038
8 years	kidney transplant	246	242	0.58	0.021
8 years	hospital dialysis	246	240	0.56	0.019
8 years	mastectomy for breast cancer	60	58	0.48	0.044
8 years	hospital confinement for an unnamed contagious disease	246	241	0.33	0.022
life	home dialysis	197	187	0.40	0.031
life	hospital dialysis	197	189	0.32	0.028
life	hospital confinement for an unnamed contagious disease	197	192	0.16	0.020
	Reference state: dead			0.00	
	Total	3 171	3 093		

Source: Drummond *et al.* (1987).

are assigned. Nevertheless many issues remain unresolved, including that of *whom* one should ask about health state preferences (patients, doctors or the general public) and that of the variability in health state valuations, both among different respondents and in different techniques. (See Torrance, 1986, for an extensive review.)

Finally, in recent years there have been attempts to obtain direct willingness-to-pay estimates for health benefits. For example, Thompson (1986) asked arthritis sufferers what they would be willing to pay, as a percentage of household income, for a complete cure. His study showed that such estimates were practically feasible, but studies are currently few in number (Donaldson, 1990). However this may signify a resurgence of true CBA, as opposed to CEA or CUA, in the health care field (Johannesson and Jönsson, 1991).

6 ANALYSIS OF DISTRIBUTIVE EFFECTS

Given the comments made earlier about the distinctive characteristics of the commodity health care, one would expect that 'CBA' in health care has paid some attention to distributive issues as well as efficiency. The departures from the classical Paretian approach to CBA have already been cited as evidence of this. In addition, concerns about equity have been cited by some analysts as the reason for their rejection of the human capital approach to the valuation of health benefits. Equity issues are also sometimes mentioned in the discussion of study results. Glass (1979) gives an excellent description of the choice (in screening for bacteriuria in school children) between a more cost-effective unsupervised test and a supervised test which gave a higher yield among children in lower socioeconomic groups.

The more recent literature has focused on the distributive issues surrounding the use of cost-utility analyses to inform health care priorities. These analyses treat the gain of a QALY as being the same no matter to whom it accrues. However it has been suggested that this discriminates against the elderly, who have fewer potential QALYs to gain from health care interventions. Concern has also been expressed that many of the treatments for end-stage disease, such as renal dialysis, appear near the bottom of the rankings and therefore, according to the analysis, should have low priority.

Some of the arguments against cost per QALY comparisons are not well formulated and it is therefore difficult for analysts to respond in a constructive manner. It is, however, widely acknowledged that health care priority setting inevitably incorporates value judgements and that, in equally weighting QALYs, analysts are taking a particular value position. The more difficult issues relate to what other value positions one could legitimately take and to the fact that, in combining cost and QALY data to generate the rankings, the 'CBA' practitioner may in fact be adopting two, possibly conflicting, value positions since the cost data derive largely from market transactions that reflect the prevailing distribution of income (Williams, 1981).

7 OTHER METHODOLOGICAL ISSUES IN 'CBA' IN HEALTH CARE

The discussion above has outlined the major methodological issues in 'CBA' in health care. For completeness it is worth mentioning the issues surrounding the adjustment of costs and benefits for differential timing (discounting to present values) and the handling of uncertainty in cost and benefit estimates.

The practice of discounting in 'CBA' in health care follows the standard conventions. The discount rates used in the literature range from 3 to 10 per cent per annum in real terms, with the majority of studies using a rate of 5 per cent. There has been some debate about the discount rate for health and whether this should be different from that for costs, or even zero (Parsonage and Neuburger, 1992; Cairns, 1992). In addition, where benefits are expressed in non-monetary units, analysts have, on occasions, not discounted them to present values. However the current convention is to discount costs and benefits by the same rate; also QALYs are always discounted.

With regard to handling uncertainty, 'CBA' practitioners in health care have developed a number of techniques, either out of necessity or as a result of working with other health care researchers. It is now common for analysts to undertake a *sensitivity analysis*, whereby the study is reworked using different assumptions for some of the key parameters. The object is to assess whether imprecision in estimation, or methodological controversy, have a significant impact on study results.

The other common approach is to couch the analysis in a decision-theoretic framework. This is particularly useful when analysing complex sequences of clinical choices, in that a medical treatment usually embodies, not one, but a series of decisions depending on how the patient responds. Construction of a decision tree comprising decision nodes and chance nodes makes the logical structure of events clear and the probabilities of particular outcomes can be varied in order to calculate the expected costs and outcomes of different decision paths under different assumptions. (See, for example, the study by Davies and Drummond, 1991.)

8 CONCLUSIONS: WHAT 'CBA' IN HEALTH AND HEALTH CARE HAS CONTRIBUTED

The contribution of 'CBA' in this field can be assessed under two headings: contributions to theory and contributions to practice. In respect of methodological development, the major contribution has been in the field of health status measurement and valuation. Faced with the problem that health care has distinctive characteristics and is normally not traded, analysts have developed ways of comparing the outputs of different health care programmes and treatments along a common dimension. These approaches may be of use in related fields where there are multiple dimensions of output, or criteria for assessing the 'success' of projects.

In practical terms 'CBA' in health care can be seen to be having a growing influence on decision making. There are some instances, admittedly few, where the final policy decision was tied quite closely to a 'CBA', such as in the decision to add immunization programmes to the services available to the elderly in the USA (Banta *et al.*, 1981) and in the decision to expand the heart transplant programme in the UK (Buxton, 1987). Also in the UK, cost-utility analyses have been undertaken as a component of government reports on breast cancer screening and opportunistic testing for elevated cholesterol. There are, in addition, other more modest instances where an economic evaluation has led to the modification of local clinical policy. However, in general, it has to be recognized that decisions depend on a number of factors and that 'CBAs' are merely an aid to decision making.

Overall 'CBA', at least in the form it is practised, has a growing influence in the health care field, but much of its acceptability results from the departure by analysts from 'classical' CBA. Indeed it could be said that 'CBA' in health care is fine in practice, and the more interesting question is does it work in theory?

ACKNOWLEDGEMENTS

The Centre for Health Economics receives a gift from the Merck Company Foundation to explore the methodological problems in conducting economic evaluations of clinical interventions. I am also Project Leader of a European Community Concerted Action on the Methodology of Economic Appraisal of Health Technology. Finally, I am grateful to Vanessa Windass for typing the manuscript.

BIBLIOGRAPHY

Akehurst, R.L. (1989), 'What can clinicians contribute to the planning of capital developments?' in R.L. Akehurst and M.F. Drummond (eds), *Clinicians and the Management of Health Care Resources*, Bristol: NHS Training Authority.

Banta, H.D., Behney, C., Willems, J. and Sisk, J. (1981), *Toward Rational Technology in Medicine*, New York: Springer and Co.

Bulthuis, R. (1984), 'Cimetidine and the cost of peptic ulcer in the Netherlands', *Effective Health Care*; 1, (6), pp. 297–309.

Buxton, M.J. (1987), 'Problems in economic appraisal of new health technology: the evaluation of heart transplants in the UK', in B. Stocking (ed.), *Expensive Health Technologies: Regulatory and Administrative Systems in Europe*, Oxford: Oxford University Press.

Cairns, J. (1992), 'Discounting and health benefits: another perspective', *Health Economics*, 1, (1), pp. 76–9.

Cohen, D. and Henderson, J. (1988), *Health, Prevention and Economics*, Oxford: Oxford University Press.

Cribb, A. and Haycox, A. (1989), 'Economic analysis in the evaluation of health promotion', *Community Medicine*, 11, (4), pp. 299–305.

Culyer, A.J. (1976), *Need and the National Health Service*, London: Martin Robertson.

Culyer, A.J. and Maynard, A.K. (1981), 'Cost-effectiveness of duodenal ulcer treatment', *Social Science and Medicine*: 15c, pp. 3–11.

Davies, L.M. and Drummond, M.F. (1991), 'Management of labour: consumer choice and cost implications', *Journal of Obstetrics and Gynaecology*, 11, (Suppl. 1), pp. 528–33.

Department of Health and Social Security (1981), *Health Services Management: Health Building Procedures*, HN(81) 30, London: DHSS.

Donaldson, C. (1990), 'Willingness to pay for publicly-provided goods: a possible measure of benefit', *Journal of Health Economics*, 9, pp. 103–18.

Drummond, M.F. (1981a), *Studies in Economic Appraisal in Health Care*, Oxford: Oxford University Press.

Drummond, M.F. (1981b), 'Welfare economics and cost benefit analysis in health care', *Scottish Journal of Political Economy*: 28, (2), pp. 125–45.

Drummond, M.F. (1987a), *Economic appraisal of Health Technology in the European Community*, Oxford: Oxford University Press.

Drummond, M.F. (1987b), 'Resource allocation decisions in health care: a role for quality of life assessments?', *Journal of Chronic Diseases*, 40, (6), pp. 605–16.

Drummond, M.F. (1990), 'Priority setting for AIDS and other health care programmes', in M.F. Drummond and L.M. Davies (eds), *AIDS: The Challenge for Economic Analysis*, Birmingham: Health Services Management Centre.

Drummond, M.F. and Davies, L.M. (1991), 'Economic analysis alongside clinical trails: revisiting the methodological issues', *International Journal of Technology Assessment in Health Care*, 7, (4), pp. 561–73.

Drummond, M.F., Lowson, K.V., Ludbrook, A. and Steele, R. (1986), *Studies in Economic Appraisal in Health Care: Volume 2*, Oxford: Oxford University Press.

Drummond, M.F., Mohide, E.A., Tew, M., Streiner, D.L., Pringle, D.M. and Gilbert, J.R. (1991), 'Economic evaluation of a support programme for care givers of demented elderly', *International Journal of Technology Assessment in Health Care*, 7, (2), pp. 209–19.

Drummond, M.F., Stoddart, G.L. and Torrance, G.W. (1987), *Methods for the Economic Evaluation of Health Care Programmes*, Oxford: Oxford University Press.

Evans, R.G. (1974), 'Supplier-induced demand', in M. Perlman (ed.), *Economics and Health Economics*, London and Tokyo: IEA.

Finkler, S.A. (1982), 'The distinction between costs and charges', *Annals of Internal Medicine*, **96**, pp. 102–9.

Fuchs, V. (1986), *The Health Economy*, Cambridge, Mass: Harvard University Press.

Glass, N.J. (1979), 'Evaluation of health service developments', in K. Lee (ed.), *Economics and Health Planning*, London: Croom Helm.

Graham, J.D. and Vaupel, J.W. (1981), 'Value of a life: what difference does it make?', *Risk Analysis*, **1**, (1), pp. 89–95.

Grossman, M. (1972), 'On the concept of human capital and the demand for health', *Journal of Political Economy*, **80**, pp. 223–55.

Helliwell, B. and Drummond, M.F. (1988), 'The costs and benefits of preventing influenza in Ontario's elderly', *Canadian Journal of Public Health*, **79**, (3), pp. 175–80.

Johannesson, M. and Jönsson, B. (1991), 'Economic evaluation in health care: is there a role for cost–benefit analysis?', *Health Policy*, **17**, 1–23.

Jones-Lee, M.W. (1976), *The Value of Life*, London: Martin Robertson.

Kind, P., Rosser, R.M. and Williams, A.H. (1982), 'Valuation of quality of life: some psychometric evidence', in M.W. Jones-Lee (ed.), *The Value of Life and Safety*, Amsterdam: Elsevier, North Holland.

Knill-Jones, R.P., Drummond, M.F., Kohli, H. and Davies, L.M. (1990), 'Economic evaluation of gastric ulcer prophylaxis in patients receiving non-steroidal anti-inflammatory drugs', *Postgraduate Medical Journal*, **66**, pp. 639–46.

Kreidel (1980), 'Cost–benefit analysis of epilepsy clinics', *Social Science and Medicine*, **14C**, pp. 35–9.

Kristiansen, I.S., Eggen, A.E. and Thelle, D.S. (1991), 'Cost-effectiveness of incremental programmes for lowering serum cholesterol concentration: is individual intervention worthwhile?', *British Medical Journal*, **302**, pp. 1119–22.

Levine, M.N., Drummond, M.F. and Labelle, R.J. (1985), 'Cost-effectiveness in the diagnosis and treatment of carcinoma of unknown primary origin', *Canadian Medical Association Journal*, **133**, pp. 977–87.

Lichfield, N., Kettle, P. and Whitbread, M. (1977), *Evaluation in the Planning Process*, Oxford: Pergamon Press.

Loomes, G. and McKenzie, L. (1989), 'The use of QALYs in health care decision making', *Social Science and Medicine*, **28**, (4), pp. 299–308.

Lowson, K.V., Drummond, M.F. and Bishop, J.M. (1981), 'Costing new services: long-term domiciliary oxygen therapy', *Lancet*, **i**, pp. 1146–9.

Luce, B.R. and Elixhauser, A. (1990), *Standards for Socio-economic Evaluation of Health Care Products and Services*, Berlin: Springer-Verlag.

Ludbrook, A. (1981), 'A cost-effectiveness analysis of the treatment of chronic renal failure', *Applied Economics*, **13**, 337–50.

Mehrez, A. and Gafni, A. (1989), 'Quality adjusted life years, utility theory and healthy years equivalents', *Medical Decision Making*, **9**, pp. 142–9.

Mills, A. (1985), 'Survey of cost-effectiveness and cost–benefit analyses in developing countries' *World Health Statistics Quarterly*, **38**, (4).

Mugarra, I. and Cabasés, J.M. (1990), 'Cost–benefit analysis of early screening for metabolic disorders in the Basque Country', *Gaceta Sanitaria*, **4**, (19), pp. 140–44.

Parsonage, M. and Neuburger, H. (1992), 'Discounting and health benefits', *Health Economics*, **1**, (1), pp. 71–6.

Russell, I.T., Devlin, H.B., Fell, M., Glass, N.J. and Newell, D.T. (1977), 'Day case surgery for hernias and haemorrhoids: a clinical, social and economic evaluation', *Lancet*, **i**, pp. 844–7.

Schweitzer, S.O. (1974), 'Cost-effectiveness of early detection of disease', *Health Services Research*, Spring; pp. 22–32.

Stason, W.B. and Weinstein, M.C. (1977), 'Allocation of resources to manage hypertension', *New England Journal of Medicine*, **296** (13), pp. 732–9.

Sugden, R. and Williams, A. (1979), *The Principles of Practical Cost–Benefit Analysis*, Oxford: Oxford University Press.

Thompson, M.S. (1986), 'Willingness to pay and accept risks to cure chronic disease', *American Journal of Public Health*, **76**, (4), pp. 392–6.

Thomson, J.L.G. (1977), 'Cost-effectiveness of an EMI brain scanner: a review of 2 year experience', *Health Trends*, **9**, pp. 16–19.

Torrance, G.W. (1986), 'Measurement of health-state utilities for economic appraisal: a review', *Journal of Health Economics*, **5**, pp. 1–30.

Torrance, G.W. and Feeny, D. (1989), 'Utilities and quality-adjusted life years', *International Journal of Technology Assessment in Health Care*, **5**, pp. 559–75.

von Neumann, J. and Morgenstern, O. (1944), *Theory of Games and Economic Behaviour*, Princeton, NJ: Princeton University Press.

Wager, R. (1972), *Care of the Elderly – an Exercise in Cost–Benefit Analysis*, commissioned by Essex County Council, London: IMTA (now CIPFA).

Warner, K.E. and Luce, B.R. (1982), *Cost–Benefit and Cost-effectiveness Analysis in Health Care*, Ann Arbor, MI: Health Administration Press.

Weisbrod, B.A., Test, M.A. and Stein, L.I. (1980), 'Alternative to mental hospital treatment: economic cost–benefit analysis', *Archives of General Psychiatry*, **37**, pp. 400–405.

Williams, A.H. (1981), 'Welfare economics and health status measurement', in J. van der Gaag and M. Perlman (eds), *Health Economics and Health Economics*, Amsterdam: North-Holland.

Williams, A.H. (1985), 'Economics of coronary artery bypass grafting', *British Medical Journal*, **291**, pp. 326–9.

Wright, K.G., Cairns, J.A. and Snell, M.C. (1981), *Costing Care*, Social Services Monographs: Research in Practice, Sheffield: University of Sheffield Joint Unit for Social Services Research.

PART III

Policy Context

7. Project Finance and Decentralization in Public Investment*

David Mayston and Gilberto Muraro

1 INTRODUCTION

The achievement of public sector efficiency, and value for money from the resources invested in public investment projects, depends not only upon knowing the appropriate appraisal and project management techniques to apply to each project (as in Mayston, above), but also upon two other key factors. The first is the *information* that is available to the investment decision makers, project managers and the subsequent managers of the assets created by the project. The extent of detailed information available to such decision makers will depend in part upon their closeness to the detailed context in which the project is undertaken. The second key factor is the nature of the *incentives* facing these decision makers to make good use of both the information and the resources that are available. As we note below, this second key factor in turn depends in part upon how the investment project is financed.

One increasingly popular method of increasing the incentive for the achievement of value for money in the public sector is that of increased *devolution* and *decentralisation* of the level at which decisions are made within the public sector. This has the effect of either moving the decision makers closer to the local context in which the resource management decisions will have their impact, or making them more clearly responsible for particular resource management decisions, or both. This process has taken place in recent years in the UK through initiatives such as the Financial Management Initiative in central government (Comptroller and Auditor General, 1986), the 'agencification' of central government activities (Ibbs, 1988) and the Local Management of Schools initiative (ERA, 1988) in the education sector. These initiatives have involved greater devolution of indi-

---

* This chapter is based in part on research work carried out by Professor Mayston under an ESRC-funded project WB04250012 on Public Capital Expenditure, Resource Management and Capital Accounting.

vidual decision making within an overall budget that is still determined by central government. However, particularly because of the 'lumpiness' of many public investment projects, and because of the traditional emphasis on the 'annuality' principle of controlling central government expenditure in cash terms through annual public expenditure rounds based upon particular fiscal years, capital expenditure does not fit easily into this process of devolution, as we discuss in more detail below.

At the level of the European Community (EC), the objective of greater European integration itself raises questions about how, and at what level, decisions on the use of public resources, including investment resources, should be made. The recent emphasis on the principle of 'subsidiarity' indicates that attention should be given to determining the lowest level within the EC at which such decisions can efficiently be made. More generally the precise division of responsibilities between central government and the local governmental units below central government, such as local authorities, regional parliaments and state or provincial governments, has been the subject of much debate in recent years in many parts of Europe, from the UK across to the former USSR. Pressures for greater local autonomy have existed at the same time as attempts at greater concentration of power in the hands of central government.

In this chapter we examine different possible forms of central government involvement in the appraisal and financing of local investment projects, including the case of complete local autonomy. Such local projects involve the use of significant amounts of public investment resources on local schools, hospitals, bridges, roads and other infrastructure assets. There is much evidence that the form of central government involvement in such local investment projects has in the past resulted in considerable inefficiencies in the use of scarce public investment resources (see, for example, AHST, 1985; Audit Commission, 1985; Mayston, 1990). Identifying the merits of different possible modes of central government involvement in the appraisal and financing of local investment projects is then an important step towards ensuring that public investment resources are utilized more efficiently in future investment decisions.

2　THE CASE FOR DECENTRALIZATION

By a local investment project we mean one whose benefits fall mainly on a specific locality. Since we will consider the issues raised by externalities and spillover effects in more detail in section 7 below, we will initially assume that all of the benefits (and disbenefits) of the project fall on the specific locality, and hence an absence of such spillover effects.

Before turning to several particular forms of central–local government involvement in project evaluation and financing, we may first identify a number of merits in the decentralization of detailed decisions on project selection. These relate especially to the attractiveness of decentralization as providing incentives for the efficient and effective use of information and resources:

a. each individual locality is likely to have the best information on its own preferences and priorities, and has an incentive to make decisions on the detailed selection of projects and on the choice between capital investment expenditure and different forms of current expenditure in line with these local preferences;
b. decentralization of decisions on detailed project selection minimizes the flow of information that is required by central government about local preferences; this is likely to result in lower costs of administration, information collection and processing, and a lower risk of information distortion in going from the locality to the centre;
c. any disagreements about project selection may be resolved locally, at often lower cost than if central government becomes involved in detailed bargaining, enquiries and project selection.

Depending on the form of project finance, decentralization of investment decision making may also achieve the following advantages:

d. each locality has an incentive to assess correctly all of the costs and benefits of each project proposal;
e. since the individual locality bears the cost of mistakes and inefficiency, it has an incentive to ensure that the projects are well managed and efficiently executed;
f. there is no incentive for the locality to manipulate the information provided to central government in order to distort investment choices;
g. the locality has an incentive to ensure an efficient total level of capital expenditure in the locality, and an optimal balance between public investment expenditure in the locality and its expenditure on current public services, such as street cleaning and the provision of teachers.

3 COMPLETE LOCAL AUTONOMY

As noted above, whether or not decentralization does achieve the additional advantages (d)–(g) depends upon the precise form of project financing. One possible method of financing local investment projects is by purely local finance, with complete local autonomy over the project selection and over the extent of finance devoted to investment projects in the locality. Such local autonomy brings with it freedom also to achieve the further possible advantage of decentralization:

h. each locality has an incentive to optimize the balance between public investment expenditure and private consumption expenditure through the intermediary mechanism of local decisions on local tax rates that finance local investment projects at the expense of local private consumption.

An important implicit assumption in the above posited advantages (a), (b) and (d)–(h) of decentralization is that local preferences are homogeneous, that is, there are no significant disagreements or conflicts of interest between different groups within the locality. While we will examine the consequences of relaxing this assumption later in this chapter, we may note here one important analytical model under which such homogeneity of local preferences is attained: that of the Tiebout model of local fiscal choice. Under our present assumption of zero externalities or spillover effects from local investment projects, each project may have many of the features of a pure *local public good*, particularly where it provides infrastructure or education services to which the local population then have a right of access. Tiebout's (1956) model involves the key additional assumption of *spatial mobility* of each locality's inhabitants between the different localities. Such geographical freedom of location for each individual then provides a public choice mechanism for the efficient selection of local public goods, such as local investment projects, by means of individuals voting with their feet until they find their most desirable location that is analogous to the market mechanism for private goods.

Such geographical mobility in particular facilitates a matching of each individual's desired balance between (1) the local services provided by local investment projects in schools and other infrastructure assets, (2) current services, such as the provision of teachers, not provided out of capital projects, and (3) the local taxes required to finance these local projects and services. Under the assumption of a continuum of localities offering different packages of services and taxes under constant returns to scale, each with the same employment opportunities, each individual has an incentive to move to the locality offering his or her ideal balance, if their current locality fails to offer it. Achieving this balance thereby attains the advantages (g) and (h) of decentralization under such local autonomy.

4 LOCAL PROJECTS WITH CENTRAL FINANCING AND APPROVAL

We may contrast the situation of complete local autonomy with that where central government makes available investment grants for financing local projects. We will consider initially the case where each locality bids for central government funding for a detailed project, and central government then subjects each proposal to central appraisal before accepting or rejecting each bid for financial support. Any such financial support that the central government gives will be tied here to the particular project that the locality has submitted.

Such 'project grants' have until recently been the prevalent form of Regional Health Authorities financing large local projects in the National Health Service in the UK and have played an increasingly important role in central–local governments in Italy. As noted by Chernick (1979):

> In the 1960s the project grant became the dominant form of assistance in the United States. Of the 370 grant-in-aid authorizations as of January 1, 1967, 280 were project grants... The number of grants was somewhat reduced in the 1970s under the impetus of revenue-sharing and the 'new federalism'. However, the project grant continues to be an important means of allocating intergovernmental aid.

In addition aid through the financing of specific projects has been an important feature of financial support for many less developed countries (LDCs), with the aid agency replacing central government in our analysis.

The effect of the financing by central government of an investment project is to reduce the effective price of the investment project to the recipient locality, down from its initial unitary value per unit of the currency invested under local autonomy towards zero in the limit. As discussed below, the resulting 'free good' nature of the capital to the recipient locality in turn encourages the locality to seek central government finance for a more lavish project than what it would propose under local autonomy.

The drop in the effective price of the project to the locality has both an 'income effect' and a 'substitution effect'. The 'income effect' is associated with a rise in the effective real income of the locality when it receives central funding for the project. This increase in real income is itself likely to cause it to seek a more lavish project than if it had to finance the project locally, as under local autonomy. If all goods and services are normal in demand, it will also wish to expand the level of other projects and public services in response to this real income increase. The same remains true at the margin if we consider also any local income taxation necessary to finance the central government project grant, so long as this taxation does not affect work incentives and the locality is a net recipient of funds from central government under the scheme.

However, in the general case, account must also be taken of the 'substitution effect' of the drop in the effective price of the project, when it receives central government financial support, on the locally desired level of the projects and services it desires. If the other local projects and local services are complementary or independent in demand with the project that receives central support, we can show that the price effect will not contradict the income effect in causing their desired demand to increase. However, if any of these other local projects or local services are (Hicksian) substitutes for the centrally financed project, the price effect will be negative and offset the income effect to some extent. In some cases the substitution effect may be greater than the income effect, so that the locally desired level of some other projects or services actually falls as a result of receipt of the central grant. Thus the receipt of a central government grant for an Olympic-size swimming pool in the locality may decrease the local desire for substitute projects, such as small swimming pools.

Similarly any complementarity between an increased investment in a given project and the revenue expenditures required to run the local assets, such as schools, to which the project gives rise will result in less of an increase in personal *per capita* consumption than would otherwise have occurred. At the limit *per capita* personal consumption may then actually fall as a result of the receipt of the central government grant.

Under a system of central government financing and approval of individual projects, the advantage (a) from involvement of the locality in bidding for projects may be achieved. However the additional possible advantages (b)–(h) of decentralization may well not be achieved under such a system. Particularly where the central financing and approval of projects involves central capital funds that are in a separate budget from devolved revenue funds for current expenditure, the 'free good' nature of capital under this system will distort local choices. Thus, whilst local project choices may be in line with local preferences given the 'free good' nature of capital they face under this system, they are not in line with the wider considerations of efficiency that (g) above involves, which would require that the locality take into account the positive cost of capital resources to society. This divergence is well illustrated by the following quotation from a chairman, of a district health authority in the UK facing the possibility of 'free' regional capital funding of projects:

> I and my colleagues learnt that, when it came to investment, there were two kinds of money – 'our' money and 'their' money. Our money came from internal sources – to tease this money out of revenue budgets was difficult, required

foresight, planning, cooperation of staff and fine judgement. 'Their' money, i.e. regional capital, was totally predictable in its timing and size, and its allocation seemed to many to depend on luck, on the marginality of the constituency, on the possibility and actuality of scandal and on the personal influence of the chairman. In an attempt to attract some of this [free regional project grant] money we... gambled for all or nothing, the schemes were extravagent in conception and often in revenue consequences. (AHST, 1985)

Many of these distortions were, if anything, even greater under the earlier system of Revenue Consequences of Capital Schemes (RCCS) that operated in the UK National Health Service (NHS) (Jones and Prowle, 1987), whereby project approval secured not only capital funding but also additional current revenue support to assist with the running costs of the new facility, thereby reducing the effective cost to the locality of the project, and its subsequent operation, even further.

5 LOCAL PROJECTS WITH CENTRAL BLOCK GRANT FINANCE

The third situation we can examine is one in which the locality does not receive a project grant on a project-by-project basis, but instead receives a block grant as an alternative form of grant-in-aid. By way of comparison, we can examine the case where the total value of the block grant is equal to the financial support which the central government gave as a project grant in the previous section, so that there is no change in the total of central government financial support, only in its form.

This represents a straightforward increase in income for the locality, compared to the situation of local autonomy without central government grants. If all local projects and services and local personal consumption are 'normal' goods or services, we will then have higher desired levels of all of these variables than in the local autonomy case. We can then show that the use of block grants, rather than project grants, involves an increase in welfare for the recipient locality. If the decisions on individual project selection are devolved to the individual locality, the additional information and efficiency advantages (b)–(f) of decentralization are attained. However the further potential advantage (g) of ensuring an efficient balance between total public capital investment and other forms of local public and private expenditure is not necessarily achieved by a block grant system that gives the locality a fixed capital sum to spend on capital projects of its own choice.

6 REASONS FOR CENTRAL GOVERNMENT INVOLVEMENT

Because of the presumption here against project grants and in favour of block grants, we need to investigate what redeeming features project grants may have as a form of central government involvement that makes them relatively common. This we can do by examining the reasons for central government involvement in local investment projects.

Equity Considerations

Whilst the Tiebout solution of local autonomy achieves the properties of market efficiency, it also achieves the market result of no income transfers between rich and poor. More affluent spatially mobile local taxpayers will leave those areas, such as decaying city centres, that attempt to increase taxes in order to tackle the economic and social problems of the lower-income groups. Instead the more affluent individuals will settle in more pleasant suburbs with lower taxes and with services more attuned to higher-income groups, thereby eroding the tax base of the inner city areas. The welfare policies of the inner city areas may also attract additional spatially mobile poorer individuals from other localities, increasing the pressure on local resources. Cities such as New York and Bridgeport, Connecticut will then face severe financial difficulties in continuing with such income redistribution policies, associated with the provision of local projects and services that benefit poorer groups more than such groups pay in tax contributions.

Central government involvement then becomes justified on equity grounds as a form of *fiscal federalism*, in order to redistribute income from rich localities to poor localities, while avoiding the above differential effects on the tax levels of the recipient local community that would erode their tax base. One reason for opting for project grants rather than block grants as a means of achieving this redistribution is a belief that there exist certain basic *merit goods* to which all localities in the country should have access. In Italy in the late 1940s and 1950s, these would have included water supply, water disposal and social housing. In a more advanced society, they may include hospital care, local secondary education, urban renewal and environmental protection measures.

If a given locality is a net loser from such geographical transfers, it may actually prefer local autonomy, although this may be modified by some degree of 'extended sympathy' by the more affluent localities for the poorer areas. Such sympathy would imply that some positive level of such transfers would result in 'Pareto-improving' redistributions (Hochman and Rodgers,

1969) that receive the support of all of the localities involved. The arguments for greater equity also need to be weighed here against the size of any deadweight loss from the distortionary effects of the taxation required to finance greater central government transfers between localities.

Informational Problems

A second reason for project grants may arise out of the informational problems that central government may have in assessing local needs for central government funds. The central appraisal of specific projects enables central government to assess the extent of local need for the project and the extent of the existing *capital stock* that is already available to service such needs. In some cases, local need may arise through their association with particular project needs, such as disaster relief or the need for urban renewal, that result from their geographical situation, rather than their general economic parameters.

In contrast, a system of block grants may be based upon *formula funding*, such that central government allocates funds to individual localities through a formula that includes parameters based upon census and other survey data of the socioeconomic characteristics of each locality. The problems involved in attempting to derive an appropriate funding formula for such block grants are discussed in Smith (1986), Carr-Hill (1990) and Mayston and Smith (1990).

Divergence between Central and Local Interests

An unwillingness of central government to devolve decision making on project selection to individual localities under block grants may also reflect the desire to maintain and extend the power and influence of central government over local government. In part this may be a reflection of the different balances of power between different interest groups that exist at central and local government level. Local investment projects provide the opportunity for local political activists to pursue projects that favour their own interest groups and to *externalize all or part of the costs* of the project on other groups in the locality, once we explicity recognize the possibility of non-homogeneous local preferences and divergent local interest groups.

Thus local governments may pursue projects which benefit the majority of local taxpayers who live in the urban conurbation around the local city, but externalize a large part of the cost of the project on inhabitants of surrounding rural areas who contribute tax revenue to the local government but make little use of the facilities the project provides. It was the avoidance of such cost externalization that led Buchanan and Tullock (1962) to support a *unanimity* rule for decision making. However, in the absence of such a unanimity rule, central governments may seek to protect their own supporters from cost externalization by local governments dominated by opposing interest groups. Conservative central governments in the UK have increasingly sought to limit the extent of locally raised finance that local authorities, particularly those in Labour control, can use for local projects and services, particularly in areas where such project expenditure may benefit lower-income groups at the expense of higher-income local property taxpayers. Central government approval of investment projects would extend such control even further.

A further illustration of a divergence of interest between central and local governments is provided by the European Commission's seeking to direct social investment funds towards groups within member states that it considers particularly needy, such as unemployed coalminers in the UK, but coming into conflict with national governments who place relatively less weight on these groups than does the European Commission. Devolving decisions on the allocation of investment funds under a block grant system to national governments would then result in at least some of these national governments spending the funds elsewhere. In contrast, earmarking the investment funds will with greater certainty ensure that they benefit the particular groups the European Commission wishes to see benefit.

Macroeconomic Considerations

Central government support for public works projects formed a major part of the New Deal policy of Roosevelt during the Great Depression of the 1930s in the USA for the reasons of local and regional Keynesian macroeconomic policy. However the question arises as to whether such project grants are a sensible tool of macroeconomic management. This involves in particular the questions (1) why opt for more public expenditure rather than more private expenditure through less taxation and less public debt, (2) why more local rather than central expenditure, (3) why more expenditure at the local level on investment rather than on general local public expenditure and (4) why more money for some definite local projects, evaluated and approved at central level, rather than general support for local investment?

The answers to these questions may include a lower import propensity and greater local employment generating propensity of many local public investment projects on constructing roads, schools and other facilities, compared to greater private consumption or greater private investment on new machinery or other assets. The additional local employment income thereby generated may also have a larger multiplier effect through lower import and savings propensities of the local authority workers who receive this income, compared to the employment income generated by general private expenditure.

The reasons for concentrating on local capital projects rather than local current expenditure, as an economic regulator, may include the seeming ease with which capital expenditure can be varied, compared to current services. Cancelling planned capital projects then deprives the local voter or worker of something he or she has not yet received, whereas cutting local current service expenditure may deprive him or her of a service or a job on which he or she has already come to rely. Cutting capital projects may also save large amounts of public expenditure through a limited number of cuts or project cancellations, whereas cuts in current services may be politically difficult to achieve so immediately on such a large scale.

However the seeming ease with which central government can use local capital expenditure as a macroeconomic regulator may hide what are in reality substantial inefficiencies in the microeconomic project management of local capital resources thereby generated. Thus the UK Audit Commission for Local Government (1985) concluded that the system of controls over local capital expenditure, in part for the purpose of macroeconomic regulation of total public expenditure, had 'contributed to wasteful investment by a combination of delays to worthwhile projects, pressure to spend before the [financial] year-end, failure to plan ahead and abrupt curbs in programmes with an associated loss of scale economies'. Similar disruptions to carefully formulated devolved investment plans were apparent in the frequent interventions by the UK central government during the 1960s and 1970s, for purposes of short-term macroeconomic management, in the investment plans of nationalized industries (see, for example, Marsh, 1978). The build-up of very large backlog maintenance and replacement needs for local authorities as a result of central government's restraint of capital investment and revenue expenditure by local authorities has also been widely criticized (for example, NEDO, 1985).

Macroeconomic control of public expenditure through the instruments of *cash limits* and *annual public expenditure determination* has in addition been an underlying reason for the retention of separate capital funds at regional rather than local district level in major public services such as the NHS. The 'lumpiness' of new capital projects, such as new hospitals, means that there are insufficient funds in cash terms to finance a new project in each locality in each financial year. Instead capital funds are retained at regional level, for local district authorities to bid for on a project-by-project basis, resulting in the 'free good' nature of the capital funds and associated problems noted above.

A system that overcomes these problems, whilst retaining the advantages of block grants rather than project grants, is discussed in Mayston (1990).

This involves the use of formula-based allocations of 'capital credits' that enhance local entitlements to future capital expenditure, while still maintaining macroeconomic control of public expenditure in cash terms.

Political and Bureaucratic Considerations

Whilst the above additional considerations may to some extent favour the funding of specific local projects rather than block grants, account must also be taken of important political and bureaucratic aspects of project finance and approval. In particular central government support for specific projects is open to short-term political manipulation, enabling central government to favour those localities where it can buy most votes through the approval of specific projects. The political motivation of central government approval for the UK Humber Bridge project immediately before a parliamentary by-election, despite later multi-million pound financial losses on the shortfall in toll revenue over interest charges to the local community, is documented in Bignell and Fortune (1984).

Indeed the higher public profile of the start of specific capital projects, and the favourable publicity that central government approval and funding of these projects can attract, may generate a political attraction towards specific project grants rather than block grant expenditure on a wide range of services and projects, even though the long-term benefit to the locality of these other forms of expenditure may be greater. An important example of such detrimental political distortion is that of the new-build bias induced by the political attractions of opening new roads, schools and hospitals, at the same time as existing capital assets are deprived of revenue funds for their efficient physical maintenance (see Mayston, 1990).

Such distortion occurs not only across different expenditure variables within a single-period governmental budget constraint. It occurs also across time periods, with the relatively short time horizons of central government political decision makers encouraging the approval of capital projects with an immediate political gain, but at a longer-term cost to the locality of operating and maintaining the resultant assets out of the locality's own revenue budget. The fact that capital costs typically fall on central government under specific project grants and operating costs fall on local government itself affects the project design each side has an incentive to support.

Thus local authorities (including district health authorities, in the case of the UK's NHS) have an incentive to bid for capital-using schemes, such as the inclusion of more advanced technology boilers in new hospitals, that save the local authority later revenue costs, such as energy costs. Central governments (or, in the case of the NHS, regional health authorities) have an incentive to cut capital costs in order to fit more projects into their available capital budgets, even though this may lead to more revenue costs, in the form of greater maintenance and other costs, later on for the local authority. The numerous distortions induced by the 'free good' nature of capital under this budgetary division are discussed in detail in Mayston (1990).

While central government politicians may have a short time horizon, the same may also be true of local politicians and local authority managers, particularly where the latter are on short-term performance-related contracts. One traditional reason for a separate capital budget in the NHS under regional health authority control has been to 'ring-fence' capital investment from the pressures which revenue funds are under in the provision of patient services. A system of block grants, that could be used either for capital expenditure or for other more immediate purposes, might then encourage local decision makers to eat up the 'seed corn' of capital that is needed to provide for the future. However the alternative system of a separate capital fund that is a 'free good' to the recipient local authority itself encourages a neglect of the maintenance of existing assets, with pressures on the local politicians or managers to spend on more urgent current services, in the belief that the resultant dilapidation of existing assets will boost the case for more 'free' new capital replacement funds to the locality.

The theory of budget-maximizing bureaucracies developed by Niskanen (1971) would also suggest that central government bureaucracies would be reluctant to devolve their budgets to local government under a block grant system. Chernick (1979, 1981) more particularly analyses a federal government bureacratic strategy of exploiting differences in each locality's offer curve to match central government support with local finance, aimed at maximizing the total expenditure inducement effect and the perceived importance of the central budget, whilst maintaining the appearance of excess demand for these funds.

7 SPILLOVERS

By a purely local investment project we mean one without (positive or negative) externalities on other localities. The precise boundaries of the locality may in some cases be set so as to achieve this condition. Large regions or metropolitan districts may have boundaries which include not only major cities but also their hinterlands that depend upon the city for communications and other infrastructure services. The current search for 'unitary' local authorities in the UK to be responsible for delivering all local authority services to a given area may achieve the zero externality condition to a large degree, although some spillover effects and cross-boundary flows may still remain.

A final possible justification for project grants rather than block grant support stems from the (positive or negative) spillover externalites that some (not purely) local projects can generate. Thus local projects aimed at pollution control, at improving the education and skills of the younger generation, at improved regional transport, or at protecting ancient monuments or beautiful scenery may benefit inhabitants in other localities as well as that where the project is located. Without specific project grants, the locality where the project would be located may underinvest in such projects through neglecting the spillover effects on these other localities. Such spillovers then provide a justification for central government involvement in investment finance and appraisal, in order to ensure that the effects of spillovers are internalized, and adequately taken into account by the investment appraisal in a consistent way across all localities undertaking public investments.

8 POSSIBLE ADDITIONAL NEGATIVE EFFECTS

Local Decision Lags and Organizational Inefficiencies

The requirement under project grants that projects be vetted by central government before funding approval is given may slow down the investment process and impose additional administrative costs in order to prepare and process the applications. Such indeed was the case when the Fund for Investment and Employment was first launched in Italy in 1982. However such a process may also require local government to look more closely at the detailed justification of the project, and to eliminate some less desirable projects sought for short-term political reasons that cannot easily pass a more formal cost–benefit test.

In contrast, the use of an explicit funding formula to allocate a block grant may eliminate both the decision lags and the incentive to devote resources to political lobbying of central government in order to maximize the probability of project funding. Decision costs of the investment decision may thereby be reduced.

Allocative Distortions

The 'free good' nature of capital under project grants encourages local authorities to overstate the local benefits and understate the external and other costs. Thus large public facilities approved and financed by central government are now creating urban traffic congestion in several Italian cities, without these effects having been adequately anticipated in the project approval (see Muraro, 1990).

Risk of Corruption

Whilst the opportunity for 'free' central government funds may bring with it the risk of corruption, opening up projects to central appraisal may in some cases reduce the risk of local corruption. Similarly international aid agencies may prefer to fund specific projects which they can then monitor, rather than hand out block grants whose funds may fail to reach intended target groups and become lost in other directions.

Loss of Autonomy for Local Government

Project grants involve less discretion and freedom for local government in making investment decisions than do block grants. However block grants, and the ability of local governments to supplement these by additional local taxation, borrowing or asset sales, have themselves been subject to increasing restrictions in the UK, through measures such as the Local Government (Capital Finance) Regulations 1990. With different political philosophies towards the control of public expenditure, and towards the need for local capital investment, the underlying political tensions between central and local governments are likely to persist. While there is a lack of consensus on the appropriate distribution of power between the two, local investment decisions are likely to remain caught up in the political conflict between local desires for more government spending on local projects and central government's desire to limit total public expenditure and restrict the powers of local authorities to make their own investment decisions.

9 CONCLUSION

It can be seen that, while the case is not all one-sided, there remains a general economic presumption in favour of block grants rather than project grants, once the equity considerations are taken to require central government involvement. It can also be seen that local investment projects involve both political and macroeconomic considerations. The requirement, under project grants, for a formal investment appraisal process, such as that in DHSS (1987), before central finance or approval is given may help to ensure that political considerations do not obscure the economic case for the project. Equally, however, the use of an explicit formula to allocate a block grant may help to reduce the short-term political element in allocating local investment funds.

Finally the design of an efficient system of decentralized decision making on investment projects requires a reconciliation of the conflicts that have frequently existed between the *macroeconomic* control of public expenditure by central government and the achievement of *microeconomic* efficiency of investment in local capital projects. Too often in the past, the former objective has been pursued at the expense of the latter. A means of reconciling the two, while providing incentives for greater efficiency than unaided local political decision making might imply, is discussed in Mayston (1990) in the context of a system that extends the scope of block grants to facilitate efficient intertemporal resource management. Achieving the potential efficiency properties of block grants for local investment projects in the real world then requires a recognition of both the political and the macroeconomic context in which such investment takes place.

BIBLIOGRAPHY

Association of Health Service Treasurers (AHST) (1985), *Managing Capital Assets in the National Health Service,* London: CIPFA.
Audit Commission (1985), *Capital Expenditure Controls in Local Government in England,* London: HMSO.
Bignell, V. and Fortune, J. (1984), *Understanding Systems Failures,* Manchester: Manchester University Press.
Buchanan, J. and Tullock, G. (1962), *The Calculus of Consent,* Ann Arbor: University of Michigan Press.
Carr-Hill, R. (1990), 'RAWP is Dead: Long Live RAWP', in A. Culyer, A. Maynard and J. Posnett (eds), *Competition in Health Care,* London: Macmillan, pp. 192–202.
Chernick, H. (1979), 'An Economic Model of the Distribution of Project Grants', in P. Mieszkowski and W. Oakland (eds), *Fiscal Federalism and Grants in Aid,* COUPE Papers on Public Economics, vol. 1, Washington DC: Urban Institute, pp. 81–103.
Chernick, H. (1981), 'Price Discrimination and Federal Project Grants', *Public Finance Quarterly,* 9, pp. 371–94.
Comptroller and Auditor General (1986), *The Financial Management Initiative,* HC 588, HMSO: National Audit Office.
Department of Health and Social Security (DHSS), (1987), *Option Appraisal,* London: HMSO.
Education Reform Act (ERA) (1988), London: HMSO.
Hochman, H.M. and Rodgers, J.D. (1969), 'Pareto optimal redistribution', *American Economic Review,* 59, pp. 542–57.
Ibbs, Sir Robin (1988), *Improving Management in Government: The Next Steps,* London: Cabinet Office.
Jones, T. and Prowle, M. (1987), *Health Service Finance,* 2nd edn, London: Certified Accountants Educational Trust.
Marsh, R. (1978), *Off The Rails,* London: Weidenfeld and Nicolson.
Mayston, D. (1990), 'Managing Capital Resources in the NHS', in A. Culyer, A. Maynard and J. Posnett (eds), *Competition in Health Care,* London: Macmillan, pp. 138–77.

Mayston, D. and Smith, P. (1990), Analysing the Need to Spend on Education', *Journal of the Operational Research Society*, **41**, pp. 125–31.

Muraro, G. (1990), 'Central Appraisal and Financing of Local Projects: Physiology and Pathology', paper presented to 46th Congress of International Institute of Public Finance, Brussels.

National Economic Development Office (NEDO) (1985), *Investment in the Public Built Infrastructure: Parts 1 and 2 – Overall Findings and Conclusions*, London: NEDC Papers.

Niskanen, W. (1971), *Bureaucracy and Representative Government*, Chicago: Aldine.

Smith, P. (1986), 'Resource Allocation by Formula', in D.J. Mayston and F. Terry (eds), *Public Domain 1986*, London: Public Finance Foundation.

Tiebout, C. (1956), 'A Pure Theory of Local Expenditures', *Journal of Poltical Economy*, **64**, pp. 416–24.

8. The Role of Analysts in the Public Investment Decision-making Process

Giacomo Pignataro

1 THE PROGRESSIVE VIEW OF THE PUBLIC DECISION-MAKING PROCESS

In 1936, the US Flood Control Act compelled the public agencies wishing to undertake flood control projects to carry out an estimation of their economic benefits and costs. The introduction of cost–benefit analysis in the public decision-making process was part of that 'progressive' movement which 'sought to introduce scientific methods and techniques into government' (Nelson, 1987, p.52).

The fundamental progressive idea was that of separating administration from politics, with efficiency as the main goal of the former. Consequently economists have been viewed as neutral technicians 'separate from politics, value judgements and other subjective and normative factors' (ibid., p.50). Politics should, then, be concerned with the expression of value judgements, while economists, as neutral technicians, use their skills to make public choices as efficient and effective as possible. Within this context, cost–benefit analysis can be considered as a decision rule which allows for selecting the most efficient alternative or, if other economic policy objectives are taken into account, the best one in pursuing these objectives. The government, conceived as a unitary entity, has to make its objectives, as well as their trade-off, explicit between them. The result will be a continuous improvement of government action enhancing the 'public interest'.

As far as the evaluation of public investments is concerned, the progressive view implies that economic valuation should focus only on the efficiency criterion, avoiding the introduction of non-economic value judgements in the analysis. Mishan, for instance, warns of the possible implications of any such widening of the scope of the analysis: 'the expertise of the analyst [could be] directed entirely to producing numerical affirmation of the policy maker's objectives' (Mishan, 1982, p.45). Mishan thinks of the efficiency criterion as backed by a sort of ethical consensus and, consequently, the economic contribution to social choices must be kept separate from politics since, in a sense, it is representative of what society prefers. The economist, then, is seen as a sort of counter-power to the political decision maker, because, since the efficiency criterion is backed by a large ethical consensus in society, its implementation is a means of expressing society's preferences against any particularism on the side of politicians.

2 SOME REMARKS ON THE PROGRESSIVE APPROACH

The progressive view seems to assume implicitly, on the one hand, that the results of the application of the evaluation methodologies can be unique or objectively determined and, on the other hand, that the analysts 'do their best' in using the evaluation criteria. Actually it is quite difficult to find an objective measure of the changes in social welfare induced by the implementation of public projects. For instance, if we think that the distributional impact of a project is relevant in evaluating changes in social welfare, we have to face all the problems related to the definition of a social welfare function and the choice of value judgements related to the interpersonal comparison of changes in individual utility (see Battiato, above). Moreover the same evaluation methodology is likely to provide different results. There are many effects of projects whose evaluation cannot be based on any objective reference (for example, intangibles or non-marketed goods). Besides the evaluation always implies an estimation of future conditions: therefore different analysts will probably provide different estimations of the costs or benefits of the same project (see Mayston, Battiato, above).

The final result of the application of a given methodology, as well as its contribution to the choice of projects, does not merely depend on its intrinsic characteristics. In other words, once there is a sort of commitment to using a pure efficiency criterion in evaluating public investments, it is still possible to have projects evaluated on the basis of extra-economic criteria. In fact, since the evaluation 'product' is not one with well defined and predetermined characteristics, there is room to carry out this evaluation in different ways, formally applying the same sort of methodology. This implies that the result must depend on the way analysts carry out evaluation, that is on the quantity and quality of information used by analysts and on the way in which they use this information for estimating the projects' effects.

Therefore analysts' independence is not assured by leaving political value judgements out of the evaluation of public investments: the absence of explicit provisions about this kind of consideration can cause the analysis to run the risk of a surreptitious introduction of those judgements. In this way the economic evaluation would really be relegated to the role of merely providing *ex ante* political choices with an *ex post* economic justification. Furthermore the important political questions would not be made explicit and any open debate would be prevented, contrary to a democratic political system's basic principles.

Therefore what can be relevant in the understanding of the results of analysts' evaluation, and of their actual role in project selection, is the analysis of the actions undertaken by the actors in the public investments decision-making process, (mainly the analysts and the decision maker), examining the outcome of the interplay between them. This approach will be of an economic nature and will be based on some behavioural assumptions about the way the analyst and the decision maker act, and on the way the institutional context and the evaluation methodologies affect their actions.

3 A MODEL OF ANALYSIS OF THE RELATIONSHIP BETWEEN ANALYSTS AND DECISION MAKERS

In the previous section, it was shown that the outcome of the assessment procedure cannot be objectively determined. Its characteristics mainly depend on the interaction between analysts and the other actors, directly or indirectly, involved in the evaluation and decision-making process.

Obviously, the institutional structure of the decision-making process creates a link between the different actors of that process. The characteristics of this link are mainly influenced by (1) the role that the formal structure assigns to each actor in each stage of the evaluation procedure; and (2) the nature of the analysts' appointment.

To explain and to make predictions about the outcome of this interaction it is necessary to find out whether or not each actor will behave according to the formal role assigned to him within the decision-making process. To do that, some behavioural assumptions are needed. The behaviour of analysts and decision makers within the formal structure of the decision-making process may be constrained in different ways. Within the context of this book, we examine how the implementation of either cost–benefit analysis or multicriteria methods affects the way analysts carry out a project's evaluation.

The Institutional Structure

Different formal evaluation procedures can be thought of to analyse the relationship between analysts and decision makers. Two characteristics of the formal structure of evaluation can be taken into account in defining possible evaluation procedures. A first characteristic is related to the institu-

The Role of Analysts in the Public Investment Decision-making Process 149

tional location of analysts. To keep things as simple as possible, we can think of the problem of distributing some fixed financial resources provided by central government to finance projects proposed by different subjects (local governments, other public agencies, and so on). Prior to the assignment of resources there is to be a comparative evaluation of the projects using, for instance, cost–benefit analysis. Analysts can then provide their support at different levels. Of all the possible alternative organizations, we will concentrate on the following:

1. there can be a central unit of analysts, whose responsibility is confined to checking that the correct procedure has been followed in the estimation of the project's impacts by those submitting the projects;
2. Alternatively, an evaluation of the different projects can be directly carried out by the central evaluation unit acting in the interest of government; only a minimum amount of information is required from those submitting projects.

The other characteristic we want to focus on is concerned with the formal nature of the evaluator's appointment: whether it is a permanent appointment (as with any other bureaucrat) or it is only temporary (as with an academic giving advice for a specific project or for a limited period of time). The formal structure of the evaluation process is relevant since it delimits the duties and rewards of the actors in that process.[1] If we try to apply the methodological approach outlined in the previous section, the actual behaviour of both analysts and decision makers is mainly motivated by the pursuit of their own interest rather than by adherence to their formal duties. They will act, then, so as to influence the outcome of the formal process to their advantage. In other words, the self-interested actors may be induced to use their official role to increase the utility level officially achieved.[2] This can be realized through unofficial and private relationships with other people involved in the decision-making process by informally exchanging services (usually information) of relevance to each other. Each actor will trade 'services' related to their official role for some 'reward' additional to the official one. Thus the kind of informal services unofficially traded depends on the formal structure and on the nature of the analyst's appointment.

Since these informal exchanges are not supported by any legal rule,[3] something different is necessary to make the exchange possible. Trust may be thought of as the substitute for legal rules in supporting the informal services dealt with above. Trust can be viewed as a sort of capital good: it needs resources for its accumulation. As we shall see later, trust may be developed both within the decision-making process – between analysts and the subjects interested in the investment decisions other than the decision maker, and between analysts and the decision maker – and outside it. The development of trust may generate tensions: trust can be used by analysts to facilitate the exchange of informal services with other participants in the decision-making process and those services may be more or less damaging to the decision maker's interests. The latter could attempt to counter these unofficial exchanges by building up trust between himself and the analysts. In this regard, the formal structure may be used by the decision maker as a means of implementing some desirable features of unofficial exchanges with analysts and, at the same time, reducing the strength of analysts' unofficial relations with other people.

The Behavioural Assumptions

As far as the behavioural assumptions are concerned, a very simple one, at the basis of economic analysis, is that the two actors in this relationship behave rationally, that is, they make their choices to maximize their own utility function.

The analysts' utility may be affected by the evaluation procedure in different ways. There are, however, two obvious ways in which the utility of analysts is affected by their work: through the reward they get from doing their work and the effort expended in doing it. As far as this latter aspect is concerned, effort can be identified with the time spent in carrying out the evaluation and with the accuracy of evaluation. The analysts' effort will then influence the quantity and quality of information provided to the decision maker to help him make his choices. It is possible to assume that analysts are averse to effort in so far as it creates disutility for them. Of course their utility function also depends on other factors, such as reputation among peers and so on.

As far as the decision maker's utility function is concerned, it is assumed, according to Public Choice Theory, that the main interest of decision makers lies in the probability of re-election.[4] The maximization of their respective utility can lead analysts and decision makers to a conflict of interests. In fact the decision maker should be interested in increasing the effort of analysts to provide the information he thinks is relevant (quantitatively and qualitatively) to the decision he is going to make, while analysts will try to minimize their effort, extracting the maximum reward from decision makers in different ways. Moreover decision makers would prefer an evaluation that supported their decisions (actually based on a political judgement) but, if analysts complied, this could generate a loss of prestige and reputation for them.

The existence of a conflict of interests within the evaluation process moves it away from the progressive concept. Analysts and decision makers do not necessarily act in a cooperative way and, anyway, they will not play complementary roles in that process. The evaluation process, may therefore, be characterized by tensions and the attempt of each actor to influence the others' actions. The analysis of the dynamics within the evaluation process can be better understood by looking at the formal structures of that process.

4 ANALYSTS AS BUREAUCRATS

The Case of Central Supervising Analysts

Let us first consider the case where the evaluation is carried out by the institution submitting the project for central financing: as mentioned above, a central unit of analysts will check the evaluation of each project. We assume that those central analysts are permanent employees of the ministry responsible for the final decision on the allocation of the financial resources. A common situation is that cost–benefit analysis is carried out by external collaborators of the agency proposing a project: usually there are professional organizations which specialize in supplying this kind of service. There is no doubt that these analysts will try to evaluate the project in such a way that it will appear the best possible according to the criteria judged relevant in assigning the fund's resources. Their payment, or at least part of it, will surely depend on the success of the financing request.

It is interesting to look at the possible relationship between 'hired' analysts and central analysts who have to check that all the procedures of the analysis have been correctly followed. The hired analysts actually act as a monitor of the information about projects transmitted to the central decision maker, verifying that relevant information is not being missed or that none of the information transmitted is being incorrectly interpreted.

Is there any incentive to develop unofficial relations between the central supervising analysts and the other analysts? Of course the experts hired by those submitting projects (hereafter called the 'local experts') have a strong incentive to create a stable relationship with their 'supervisors' to neutralize any possible opposition to their estimates. In this way the probability of their projects being financed is enhanced, as is their reputation in the market for the evaluation services. On the other side of this potential relationship, the supervisors may also derive some sort of benefit, which may take different forms: whereas, for instance, the evaluation procedure suggests different possible ways of estimating some projects' effects, the fact that local analysts will adopt one estimation methodology rather than another could make the supervisors' work easier or could satisfy their 'ideological' commitment to some specific methodology. An extreme form of benefit would be money: supervisors may be bribed by local analysts for their favourable opinion.

The informal exchanges between local analysts and central supervising analysts may be successfully implemented since they usually are the most 'stable' actors of the whole decision-making process: this is a favourable situation for the accumulation of trust which is at the basis of informal exchanges.

The central decision maker may be aware of the potential collusion between central and local analysts and consequently react, trying to establish a vertical network with the central supervising analysts so as to improve the quality of information about projects transmitted to him. One possibility is the manipulation of the formal structure of the bureau: reorganization is, in other words, a way of making 'payments' to central analysts. The possibilities of reorganization are, however, quite limited since the central bureau of analysts will not usually be very extensive. In fact one of the usual forms of reorganization, through the creation of new supervising levels to enhance the possibilities of promoting analysts (as a 'payment' for better information about projects), cannot, in this case, be pushed very far. But, since the central supervisory unit is a bureau of a ministry, analysts may be promoted to other bureaus of the same ministry. This way of 'paying' for the informal services provided by analysts is not easily implemented, mainly because of the resistance that may be met in those other bureaus. Therefore another way of reducing the inefficiencies connected with the existence of horizontal networks lies in their 'destruction' through the movement (without promotion, in this case) of analysts from the central supervisory bureaus to other bureaus in the same ministry. It is worth stressing, however, how the use of all these instruments by the decision maker is constrained by the usually temporary nature of his position. Hence there is a higher probability of horizontal rather than vertical trust.

As far as the results of evaluation are concerned, there is no clear-cut way of showing that, for instance, the projects' selection will be biased towards allocative efficiency or distributive justice. It is instead possible to say that the informational relevance of systematic evaluation is played down since, as has been shown, it is not easy to reduce the strength of horizontal networks. The outcome of this process will be very poor, in terms of its informational content, because of the potentially strong influence of the information provided by analysts acting in the interest of those competing for the allocation of the financial resources.

The Case of Central Evaluators

The other formal structure of the evaluation process mentioned above is one in which evaluation is carried out completely at a central level. Analysts then do not simply check that the procedure has been correctly followed: they do their own cost–benefit analysis of all the projects submitted for evaluation. Therefore they will need a lot more information than in the previous case and, perhaps, than that provided at the time the projects were proposed. Of course the best source of information for evaluating a project is the agency proposing that project. For instance, if a local council asks for financing of a project for a new road, it will probably know the potential demand for the new road better than anyone else. Therefore the central evaluation unit can get this 'input' for its cost–benefit analysis quite easily from the local council and analysts will save on their own time and effort. The council, however, has an interest in providing an overestimated figure in order to increase the amount of benefits it claims for its project. Then an informal exchange may be implemented between central evaluators and local governments: the former get the information they need at a low cost while the latter obtain a favourable evaluation of their projects. However the ability to collect relevant and useful information is not spread equally among local governments. It is probable that big local councils provided with research units will be more capable than small local councils of producing information for central evaluators which is as relevant and detailed as they need. In the end, perhaps, this evaluation structure may represent an incentive for all the local governments to improve their system of collecting information because, in that way, they can increase the probability of gaining access to a horizontal network.

Here again, the central decision maker's attempt at building vertical networks will meet the same sort of difficulties envisaged above.

5 ANALYSTS AS EXTERNAL CONSULTANTS

Different outcomes from the ones described earlier may be predicted when the analysts operating at the central government level are not bureaucrats, but have only a temporary appointment in the public sector administration. The possibility of establishing horizontal informal exchanges with other actors in the public investment decision-making process is, in this case, severely limited by the temporariness of analysts' appointments, inasmuch as an investment in the accumulation of trust is now less likely to be profitable. Moreover the existence of a horizontal network can influence the results of a project's evaluation in such a way as to damage the investment in reputation made by analysts within their profession.

There is, on the contrary, an incentive for analysts to strengthen their relations with their profession, since exchanges within it can be almost costlessly supported by the trust already accumulated. An informal exchange of information can probably be observed between analysts and their colleagues, from whose professional expertise analysts will try to benefit in carrying out the projects' evaluation: this information transfer from the profession to analysts need not be matched by some other contemporaneous service in the opposite direction, since it can be based on an already established exchange line (in other words, it compensates some services already provided by analysts or could be compensated by some services in the future).

The non-existence of horizontal networks within the decision-making process does not necessarily mean that the system of collection and communication of information is efficient from the decision maker's point of view. In fact the public nature of information about the projects' evaluation obviously related to the exchange of information between analysts and their colleagues may be negatively valued by the decision maker. However he will meet even more difficulties than before in enhancing vertical trust to reduce the influence of horizontal trust. It is, in fact, hard to contrive some sort of 'payment' to temporarily hired professionals, realized through a reorganization of the formal structure of the evaluation unit. Probably the only available instrument, in this case, is the control of appointments.

First of all, the decision maker can remove analysts from their appointed positions whenever he thinks that the horizontal ties with their profession and with the general public is very costly for him. Moreover, since he is not able to create vertical trust, he could appoint people with whom trust already exists. This last situation may well create a conflict of 'loyalties' for analysts appointed in this way: the loyalty to the decision maker and the loyalty to their profession. Of course there is no unique way of solving such a conflict. Each analyst will find his own trade-off and will act accordingly.

6 COST–BENEFIT ANALYSIS V. MULTICRITERIA METHODS

If there is no 'objective' way of carrying out an economic evaluation of public investments, something which reflects the 'true' preferences of society, then the evaluation results cannot have any normative attribution in the decision-making process.

The economic evaluation of projects may rather have an informational relevance (see Rizzo, below): first of all, it helps to take into account, in a systematic way, all the relevant effects of a project. Cost–benefit analysis, as well as other evaluation methodologies, can, in fact, be viewed as a methodological scheme to evaluate public projects provided their effects are

The Role of Analysts in the Public Investment Decision-making Process 155

previously identified. They are, therefore, techniques for the identification of the main impacts of a project, for their measurement and estimation, making possible a comparison among different projects and, consequently, a 'rational' choice.

Moreover the implementation of an analytical evaluation tool may be a means of making explicit the value judgements needed to estimate some projects' impacts. Even if a pure efficiency criterion is adopted, its implementation will in fact require the assumption of some value judgements. For instance, the choice of a social discount rate implies a value judgement about the most preferred rate of capital accumulation in society and the public sector's contribution to this accumulation (see Battiato, above). The use of an evaluation methodology may be seen as a contribution to the elucidation of choices to the general public, making control over decisions taken by politicians easier.

However the above-mentioned informational relevance of a systematic evaluation of projects and its positive contribution to rational decision making cannot be regarded as an automatic result of the implementation of an evaluation procedure within the public decision-making process. They should rather be viewed as desirable features of that procedure. Thus the problem arises of finding out about the characteristics of the evaluation procedure likely to implement those features.

We have already analysed how different formal structures of the evaluation process may influence the evaluation's results. A related aspect is the choice of the evaluation methodology to be used. Apart from the issue of which methodology is more suitable to provide useful information for choosing (see Rizzo, below), there is another question: whether the specific characteristics of each evaluation methodology are of any relevance to the analysis of the analysts' work carried out in the previous sections. In other words, is there any intrinsic characteristic of each evaluation methodology which can delimit what the analysts can do and what they are asked to do, as for the formal structure?

Cost–benefit analysis has a quite firm theoretical framework represented by Paretian Welfare Economics. Moreover, there is a complete set of established economic principles, which serve as a guide in the various steps of the application of cost–benefit analysis to the evaluation of projects. Therefore CBA provides a good basis for real competition in the production of information and for a better control of the analysts' work. Every value put into a cost–benefit calculus must be supported by an economic justification: even if there is not any objective economic justification, different opinions on that can be compared on the basis of the same economic principles, of which those opinions represent different applications. Besides, whenever the politician's choice is different from the one suggested by analysts, it can offer a genuine alternative point of view even if it is partial in its nature, since it values projects only on the basis of the efficiency criterion.

Unlike CBA, multicriteria analysis does not adopt an external theoretical reference such as Paretian Welfare Economics as the basis of evaluation. The valuation of projects largely depends on the weights attributed by the decision maker to the different criteria: it contributes to make those weights explicit (see Munda *et al.*, above). This implies that a particular valuation has to be justified only on grounds of the subjective weights of a decision maker. Alternative valuations cannot be compared with each other, since they are based on different subjective value judgements which, by definition, are not comparable. As Munda *et al.* point out, the analyst must interact with the decision maker who is regarded as the 'client' of the former. Therefore multicriteria methods allow for a collusion between analysts and decision makers as a normal feature of the evaluation process.

Of course, what has been said above does not mean that CBA cannot be used as a means of collusion between analysts and other actors in the decision-making process. Whenever the evaluation is subjectively founded, then, there is the possibility of introducing value judgements favoured by the decision maker.

CONCLUSION

It has been shown that different formal structures of the evaluation procedure, implying different divisions of responsibility within the public investment decision process, may be relevant in identifying the main tensions around the analysts' work and the possible biases it may be subject to. If the informational content of the analysts' evaluation is stressed as its most valuable characteristic, then we should prefer that formal procedure which has the potential to generate more competition of interests among the participants in the decision-making process. On the basis of the foregoing analysis, it appears that the position of external consultants may mean little interest being shown in colluding with politicians and the institutions proposing the projects. However, even if external consultants may be able to provide information on projects which is not biased by informal exchanges with the other actors in the decision-making process, this information is relevant to the general public only if the latter knows it. Therefore what is also required is public awareness of the work done by analysts in evaluating different projects, which would help to compel the decision maker to make explicit the reasons for making a decision different from the one advised by analysts.

In conclusion, we would only like to stress again the main argument of this chapter, which is the need to go beyond a sort of 'anecdotal' literature to study all those aspects related to the way analysts carry out their job, which may serve to improve the public investments decision-making process.

NOTES

1. The following analysis largely draws upon the theory of bureaucracy by Breton and Wintrobe (1982).
2. We are talking about utility levels since actors could either increase their official reward or, with the same reward, reduce their effort.
3. There is no rule compelling the party not fulfilling his obligation to obey.
4. We are implicitly assuming that the final decision maker is an elected politician.

BIBLIOGRAPHY

Allen, W. (1977), 'Economics, Economists and Economic Policy: Modern American Experiences', *History of Political Economy*, 9, (1), pp. 48–88.

Breton, A. and Wintrobe, R. (1982), *The Logic of Bureaucratic Conduct*, Cambridge: Cambridge University Press.

Goldenberg, E.N. (1983), 'The Three Faces of Evaluation', *Journal of Policy Analysis and Management*, 2, pp. 515–25.

Hanke, S.H. and Walker, R.A. (1974), 'Benefit–Cost Analysis Reconsidered: An Evaluation of the Mid-State Project', in *Benefit–Cost and Policy Analysis*, Chicago: an Aldine Annual.

Haveman, R.H. (1977), 'Policy Analysis and the Congress: An Economist's View', in R.H. Haveman and J. Margolis (eds), *Public Expenditure and Policy Analysis*, 2nd ed., Chicago: Rand McNally, pp. 577–91.

Mishan, E.J. (1982), 'The new Controvesy about the Rationale of Economic Evaluation', *Journal of Economic Issues*, XVI, (1), March, pp. 29–48.

Nelson, R.H. (1987), 'The Economics Profession and the Making of Public Policy', *Journal of Economic Literature*, XXV, pp. 49–91.

Niskanen, W.A. (1986), 'Economists and Politicians', *Journal of Policy Analysis and Management*, 5, (2), pp. 234–44.

Pechman, J.A. (ed.) (1989), *The Role of the Economist in Government*, New York: Harvester Wheatsheaf.

9. The Public Decision-making Process and Cost–Benefit Analysis

Ilde Rizzo

1 INTRODUCTION

In the economic literature the evaluation of public investment is a much debated issue. The theoretical issues involved in the evaluation of public projects are outside the scope of this chapter and are extensively examined in the first part of this book. The aim of this chapter is merely to explore the relationship between cost–benefit analysis (CBA) and the public decision-making process. Attention will also be paid to the impact of the multicriteria approach (MCA) on such a process.

The main features of the public decision-making process will be recalled and connected with the crucial steps usually encountered in the application of CBA. The idea is that the characteristics of the public decision-making process permit the participants to circumvent the 'objectivity' of CBA and ensure the representation of the intensity of preferences. At the same time, the systematic application of evaluation techniques might affect positively the functioning of the process itself, because the information is improved. From this point of view, the impact of CBA and MCA on the public decision-making process will be compared.

The analysis develops as follows: in section 2 the main features of the public decision-making process will be recalled to examine the interaction between them and the application of CBA. In section 3 a comparison will be drawn between CBA and MCA as far as their impact on public decision making is concerned. Some concluding remarks will be offered in section 4.

2 THE PUBLIC DECISION-MAKING PROCESS AND CBA

Some Preliminary Remarks

CBA may be considered a test of 'social profitability'. Many controversial problems arise when the role of CBA is defined in details. The major controversy may be summarized as follows: on the one hand, some scholars (for example, Mishan 1982) argue that CBA should follow, as much as possible, market evaluations and pursue only strictly economic objectives, avoiding value judgements (this might be called the 'strict Paretian approach'); on the other hand, others argue that 'weights' and 'values' should be introduced in the evaluation process. If this is not the case, as Tresch (1981, p. 541) points out, CBA would be restricted to determining the 'relative' efficiency of a project but not its contribution to social welfare (this might be called the 'decision-making approach').

This chapter is not aimed at entering this ongoing debate, which is widely explored in the first part of this book, but at enlarging the scope of the analysis, taking into account the links which exist between CBA and the political and bureaucratic structures involved in its implementation. Such an analysis might contribute to building a 'bridge' between the 'strict Paretian' and the 'decision-making' approaches. The analysis of the political process might cast some doubts on the existence of a 'neutral' public decision maker and, therefore, would stress the abstract features of the former approach. At the same time, caution might be suggested in accepting the 'paternalistic' implications of the latter.

More precisely, the analysis will be aimed at verifying whether the coherence of CBA is affected by the features of the political process and/or whether the use of such evaluation techniques interferes with the functioning of such a process.

The Coherence of Choices

A first issue to be explored is whether and to what extent the choices deriving from CBA are affected by the organizational structure and by the degree of communication existing within the public sector. The various dimensions of such an issue are extensively explored elsewhere in this book (see Battiato, above); here only a few points will be raised.

As Dasgupta, Sen and Marglin (1972) have pointed out, those who evaluate a project have to know how the other fiscal instruments (tariffs, taxes, licences) are used by the other branches of public administration. Whether they are able to influence other branches' behaviour or whether communication does exist among the different branches of public administration greatly affects the evaluation of the project itself. The closer the relationships among bureaucracies, the higher the internal coherence of CBA evaluation is likely to be.

Moreover, whenever political evaluations are introduced to replace market evaluations, they ought to be applied in a coherent way in all the fields of government activity if the objectives underlying CBA are to be pursued. For instance, the definition of appropriate 'shadow prices' depends both on the range of economic policy instruments available to the decision maker and on the extent to which he actually uses them. As Walsh and Williams (1971) have pointed out with respect to the 'shadow prices' in the labour market, if the various decision makers adopt the same 'shadow prices', job creation in less developed areas, with unemployment above the average, would be more effectively put in to practice.

This type of problem can be solved from the operational point of view with a system of 'national parameters' to be used for all decisions connected with single projects and independent of these (see Battiato, above). Such a solution, however, is not always adopted in practice. For instance, in Italy, of the whole set of parameters, only the social rate of discount has so far been established and made compulsory. For the estimation of 'shadow prices', reliance on official 'Directives', rather than the provision of clear guidelines, has been a source of serious ambiguities. As a consequence, substantial inconsistencies may arise.

Analogous problems arise in other countries. In the UK, 'shadow prices' are not recommended and no instructions have been issued by the Treasury. According to Florio (1990), the evidence offered by Great Britain seems to suggest that the government has limited control over its agencies – because of the organizational complexity, information asymmetries and multicriteria decision making in the public sector – and that, as a consequence, inconsistencies are likely to arise in the application of CBA.

Alternative Models of the Public Decision-making Process

Another question to be answered is whether the attainment of welfare maximization (which is the object of CBA) is affected by the features of the public decision-making process. From this point of view, different models of the political process are to be compared.

According to the model implicitly underlying welfare economics, citizens entrust the decision maker to choose the most effective and suitable tools to maximize social welfare. An omniscient and benevolent planner is assumed to exist, whose only purpose is to pursue social efficiency, that is the satisfaction of individual preferences. This model is theoretically coherent with the philosophy underlying CBA; in such a case, as Randall (1985) has pointed out, CBA becomes a planning tool, to pursue the maximization of the social welfare function.

If an alternative description of the public decision-making process is adopted, so that the various participants to this process are assumed to be own-utility maximizers, a different model is needed. In this case, the analysis of the interaction between CBA and the political process is not straightforward; as Mueller (1987) has pointed out, even within a public choice perspective no unique conceptualization of the political process exists. Broadly speaking, a 'demand-oriented' and a 'supply-oriented' approach can be identified. According to the former, public policies are reflections of the preferences of individual voters and/or groups and the political process is synthesized by a voting rule transforming their preferences into political outcomes. On the other hand, the latter approach places the government above the citizens, stressing that it is the preferences of the individuals in the government that are decisive, because politicians and bureaucrats pursue their own interests.

As Mueller (ibid., pp. 142–3) has argued, 'both views might be correct to some degree. Government officials and bureaucrats may have discretionary power to advance their own interests at the citizens' expense to some degree, but citizens' preferences, as registered through existing political institutions, may also constitute a consequential constraint'. Empirical investigation does not provide unambiguous answers as far as the explicative power of the above mentioned models is concerned; according to Mueller (ibid., p.143), the most important public choice message is that 'institutions matter' and strongly affect political outcomes.

On the grounds of the above considerations, far from choosing one conceptualization or the other it seems preferable to describe the public decision-making process as adopting a broad public choice framework, based on the concept of exchange, the outcome of which, however, is an open question. Voters, individually or through their interest groups, try to influence public choices. Own-utility maximizer legislators and bureaucrats are the other parties involved. Voters' preferences may or may not weigh with the legislators who take decisions. The decisions are put into effect by bureaucrats, who may be more or less effective and whose interests may not necessarily coincide with society's preferences. In other words, conflicts of interests are likely to exist. The legislators may be constrained by the preferences of the electorate (through the need for re-election) but their goals may differ from those of their constituents. At the same time, the objectives of those who implement legislation may diverge from those of voters or politicians. As a consequence, divergent objectives, other than the maximization of social welfare, may be worked out.[1] The crucial issue, then, is to verify to what extent citizens are able to induce government to be truly 'representative', that is efficient.

Alternatively the decision-making process can be described as a network of principal–agent relationships:[2] electorate/elected public officials, elected public officials/bureaucracy, characterized, as usual, by asymmetrical information. The issue, then, again, is to identify proper means to induce the agent to work in the interest of the principal.

CBA and Intragovernmental Competition

Interesting insights in this direction may be derived from the concept of intragovernmental competition put forward by Breton (1987) and extensively explored by many scholars. Intragovernmental competition is the competition that originates in the 'checks and balances' which characterize governmental systems.[3] The existence of 'checks and balances' is assumed to reduce the degree of freedom for public decision makers and to provide them with incentives towards a good performance, similar to those existing, *mutatis mutandis*, in competitive markets. External controls are likely to induce more efficient (both technically and allocationally) behaviours, leading, for instance, to the choice of the most effective instrument (given the object to be pursued) rather than to the less 'politically expensive'. As a consequence, popular control over the exercise of political power is likely to be enhanced; it is claimed that 'checks and balances, by raising the level of political involvement on the part of citizens, increase the legitimacy of the political process' (Breton, ibid., p. 286).

A detailed analysis of such an approach is outside the scope of this chapter;[4] what matters here is to stress how and why such a concept is relevant for the issue under study. As is well known, no matter whether we talk of the Schumpeterian 'entrepreneurial competition' or of 'price competition', we have in mind competing agents; the behaviour of each competitor affects the others' and the effect is the consumer's greater satisfaction. In the long run profit-seeking entrepreneurs generate a dynamic process of reallocation of resources; neither extra-profits nor quasi-rents can accrue to the entrepreneur because they are extracted by others competing for them.

When transferred to the political arena these considerations imply that each actor in the political process can induce the others to behave according to (allocational and technical) efficiency rules. Indeed the degree of freedom of each decision maker is reduced and, therefore, the possibility of gaining personal rewards is curtailed, because institutional bodies do not carry out their own functions enjoying a monopolistic position. The introduction of evaluation procedures, such as CBA might be viewed as *innovation* in Schumpeterian terms, that is implementation of new programmes, policies, techniques of administration and a way to promote competition within government, comparable to the more traditional 'checks and balances' mentioned above.

As Breton and Wintrobe (1982) point out, *inventions* such as CBA do not originate with bureaucracy but from citizens' groups, academics and social critics. Entrepreneurship is to implement them; in the Schumpeterian world, entrepreneurial innovation is the driving force of competition, implying emulation by others of the entrepreneur's innovation. *Mutatis mutandis*, in a public sector environment, such an argument implies the spread of innovations, though originated by different motivations and the development of competition.

Further insights in this direction may be derived by looking at empirical evidence, in the light of the analyses developed in Chapters 7 and 8. In Italy, since 1982, the Unit for the Evaluation of Public Investments (*Nucleo di Valutazione degli Investimenti Pubblici* – NVIP) operates within the Ministry of Budget and Planning, with the purpose of allocating the newly born Investment and Employment Fund (*Fondo Investimenti Occupazione* – FIO). It seems significant that, after the creation of NVIP, other new bodies have been set up, within different ministries but with analogous terms of reference. For instance, investment projects for Southern Italy are subjected to the evaluation of a specific body, created for this purpose within the Department for Southern Italy. At the same time, the projects referring to environmental problems are examined not only by NVIP but also by an analogous body, established within the Ministry of the Environment. Moreover it is also interesting that Evaluation Units have been established in many regions, too; according to a recent survey of regional spending legislation (Florio, 1990), between 1984 and 1988 two-thirds of Italian regions introduced programme and project appraisal in the evaluation of capital expenditure. In Schumpeterian terms the increasing attention paid by various branches of the executive, at various levels of government, to the adoption of evaluation techniques seems to suggest that the entrepreneur's rents are competed away by imitators. Whether the policies adopted are successful depends on their institutional and organizational features and does not alter the fact that competition seems to be expanding.

If the analyst and decision maker roles are strictly independent and separated, decisions may be transparent, making the decision takers accountable to public opinion (see Pignataro, above). In such an ideal situation intragovernmental competition is likely to occur because different departments compete with each other to obtain funds;[5] the Economic Planning Committee (CIPE) and the Cabinet, who ultimately decide the allocation of FIO, are subject to the external check deriving by the fact that the determinants of their political choices are made clear by the adoption of CBA.

Looking at the empirical evidence, however, some comments are in order. According to Pennisi and Peterlini (1987) NVIP is characterized by 'institutional ambiguity', which has strongly undermined its performance. More precisely it has been claimed that NVIP has been conceived to increase the relative 'weight' of the Ministry of Budget and Planning with respect to the Treasury and that such a 'risk' has been avoided by confining the NVIP to the allocation of the FIO rather than giving it a wider scope. The institutional features of such a body are, indeed, very much debated. Rather than being a technical body with external relevance, it has been conceived as an internal committee (within the above-mentioned ministry), reporting directly to the politicians. Its brief history has been characterized by various crises, and conflicts both within the NVIP (that is, among its members) and in the relationship between NVIP itself and the politicians and the bureaucratic management of the ministry. As a result, rather than being an instrument for ensuring transparent decisions, attempts have been made to transform it gradually into a means to 'legitimate obscure political decisions' (see the 'justificing' behaviour in Munda *et al.*, above).

Nevertheless, from the intragovernmental competition point of view, the evaluation of such an experience may be less pessimistic. In fact it may be considered a first step towards the improvement of public decision-making procedures; moreover it is a good example to test for the difficulties to be overcome bringing government under control and an indirect confirmation that institutions matter.

CBA and Intergovernmental Competition

Further insights may be introduced when the existence of different levels of government is taken into account. In this perspective, exchanges take place not only between citizen and legislators but also between central and local governments. An example may throw some light on this issue.

Let us consider an investment regarding natural resources, the benefits of which accrue at sub-central level while the costs are borne at central level. The citizens living in the sub-central area clearly support the project, even if its net real benefits are dubious. Central government choice, therefore, might be determined more by the different intensity and political influence of local demands than by the relative economic convenience of various projects. As has been pointed out by Haveman (1980), this kind of situation recalls the problems encountered in the exploitation of 'common property'. In fact central government funds can be considered similar to a common good which provides specific benefits to a well defined local area at the expense of a wider community.[6]

CBA might turn out to be a useful instrument to introduce competition between governments. In fact, to bring the process described above somehow under control, local government projects should be submitted to the central authority for approval only if accompanied by the test of CBA. Such a procedure would make them comparable on a technical basis and would reduce political discretion. It might be argued that this is likely to introduce a bias against the less developed local governments, under the assumption that administrative efficiency is positively related to the local income level. As a consequence, poor areas, having less efficient organization and evaluation structures might be penalized in the allocation of resources, even if their projects are 'intrinsically' more convenient. Therefore, in the short run distributional problems might arise in the allocation of funds; however, in the long run, incentives towards the rationalization of decision making might be introduced. In fact local representatives have to face their voters' control, expecially if the local administrative inefficiency of a constituency leads to its 'penalization' in the allocation of funds.

On the other hand, in practice, local organizational inefficiencies, corruption and allocative distortions might arise as a consequence of central appraisal of local projects: local governments have a strong incentive to increase artificially the net benefit resulting from the project formulation, increasing the benefits and/or hiding the costs. Such behaviour, however, may be discouraged if the relevance of local government credibility is stressed and unreliable behaviour penalized, even if implicitly. Moreover, as Muraro (1990) points out, local authorities, to increase the probability of obtaining funds, can present central government with a *fait accompli*, i.e. anticipating part of the work, with costs just a little higher than the initial excess of costs over benefits. If a project can be submitted repeatedly, such a strategy is implicitly encouraged. Again, as has been stressed above, what seems to be crucial is the institutional and procedural solution chosen.

Political Constraints

The fact that the functioning of the public sector differs from the abstract model usually described in welfare economics does not necessarily imply that CBA should not be used. Indeed its principles may still hold and, given the existing political constraints, may be applied to find the most convenient solution.

Examples of the influence exerted by political constraints on CBA are provided by Gramlich (1981) with respect to the USA experience; nevertheless they offer useful general insights. For instance, it is argued that when the financial year is about to finish, each department tries to reduce as much as possible the residuals, to avoid the possibility of its funds being cut in the next year on the grounds that residuals are available to be spent. To achieve this object, departments increase their spending activity, even financing projects which are not profitable from the CBA point of view.

Another example is provided by the existence of so-called 'sacred cows', government projects which, being very popular, are considered as given and 'untouchable' by politicians, even if their social profitability is far from being seriously demonstrated. A similar form of political bias is also likely to arise in favour of the projects with concentrated benefits and dispersed costs, since the intensity of the preferences for the gainers is greater than for the losers.

Moreover Margolis (1980) and Haveman (1980) argue that the positive analysis of bureaucratic behaviour would stress the shortcomings of CBA as an evaluation method. According to these studies difficulties arise in applying CBA properly whenever the rationality of the choice conflicts with bureaucrats' utility function. These difficulties are exemplified by arguing that administrators exhibit a positive bias toward low discount rates and/or that they fail to take into account all the relevant alternatives. The above arguments, however, lose relevance if a distinction is drawn between technical and political choices. For instance, as Peacock (1973) has stressed, the choice of relevant evaluation parameters such as the rate of discount can be made political and, indeed, this is the solution adopted in some countries, for example, Italy, as was pointed out above.

Further political constraints arise from the existence of imperfections in the 'political market', as far as the diffusion of information is concerned. Fiscal illusion,[7] in fact, is likely to have relevant effects on the evaluation of projects. For instance, regardless of the real net benefit involved in each investment, decision makers might prefer those exhibiting benefits which are more 'visible' than costs. Haveman (1980) has argued that whenever divergences do exist between the decision maker's and society's utility functions, the former might try to manipulate the degree of visibility of the benefits and costs related to the various projects, according to its own utility function. Such behaviour is made possible by the functioning of the 'political market'; it might imply that funds are allocated to projects which are not very convenient from the social point of view.

Strangely enough, however, it is the existence of the above-mentioned constraints that provides useful arguments to support the utilization of CBA. In fact, in the absence of any systematic method of evaluation and control, public decisions might become dominated by the conflicts of interest. Considering the application of CBA in the area of water resources in the USA, Campen (1986, pp.86–7) has pointed out that the agencies involved have tried to distort CBA to their own ends but the relevant question is: how are things different from what would have happened in the absence of such a technique? 'An examination of the historical record indicates that cost–benefit analysis has played a role in ... reducing the number of ill-conceived pork-barrel water resources projects adopted.'

In a public choice perspective, therefore, as Randall (1985) has also pointed out, the role of CBA appears to be well defined: rather than a decision-making tool it seems to be an informative system for public opinion, which turns out to be a useful instrument to deal with the 'second best' problems (see Battiato, above) derived from the existence of political constraints. Its major scope may be envisaged in the reduction of asymmetrical information, characterizing the relationships underlying public decision making, by ensuring a more homogeneous distribution of the available information. Depending on the institutional features, such a technique may positively affect the responsiveness, that is the efficiency, of the public decision-making process, increasing the accountability of the political decision maker: citizens' control over politicians is enhanced and, on the other hand, better informed politicians are likely to constitute an incentive towards good performance for bureaucrats.

The adoption of rational criteria of evaluation such as CBA might, therefore, induce positive changes, at least in the long term, in public sector decision making. It is true that CBA tends frequently to reflect particular interests and that it leaves scope for potential abuse and misuse; such a tendency might be effectively countered by ensuring that all groups with significant interests in the outcome of a decision are represented, in other words by improving the informative system underlying public decision making. For instance, a useful step in this direction might be taken through the regular publication of official reports giving details of the evaluation decision-making process, ensuring transparency and publicity of public decisions and, therefore, drawing public attention to such a process.

3 MULTICRITERIA ANALYSIS AND THE PUBLIC DECISION-MAKING PROCESS

The impact of CBA on the public decision-making process having been sketched, let us briefly examine how such an impact differs if other evaluation techniques are used; from this specific point of view, our attention will be devoted to multicriteria analysis (MCA), the main features of which have been extensively explored in Chapter 3 of this book. It is argued that MCA transcends the narrow boundaries of CBA's single indicator, extending the evaluation, among other things, to intangibles and to distribution issues. The point to be considered here is whether in so doing MCA is likely to improve, from the citizens' point of view, the results of the public decision-making process.

MCA implies an interactive decision support system the aim of which is to help the decision maker during the evolution of the decision process. Emphasis, then, is placed on the process itself rather than on its results alone. And in fact, MCA, unlike CBA, does not come up with a single money indicator but, once objectives are defined, at each step identifies a new non-dominated solution, each one assigning specific weights to the different objective, until a satisfactory (for the decision maker.) compromise among the different objectives is reached.

If the public decision-making process is unbiased, that is if the interests of the various actors converge towards the maximization of social (not only strictly economic) welfare, it might be argued that MCA is an improvement over CBA, since the scope of the evaluation is enlarged. If, on the other hand, as has been pointed out, the decision-making process is potentially biased, the answer is less straightforward. In theory, MCA allows for a greater production of information, the emphasis posed on the process itself seems to ensure transparency and, therefore, to allow for a greater external control on the decision making.

In other words, the role of project evaluation as informative support, to reduce asymmetrical information, might be stressed. Whether information does, indeed, reach the public is another question, mainly depending on the institutional solution chosen, that is on the type of institutional relationship linking the analyst and the decision maker. The relevance of this point has already been stressed with respect to CBA and this issue is extensively dealt with in this book (see Pignataro, above). Here it will suffice to stress that, if the relationship between the decision maker and the analyst is such that information does not become available outside, MCA is likely to reinforce the bias of the public decision-making process. The decision maker's discretion is less constrained than in the CBA case, given that in pursuing his own interests he will not be constrained by the economic efficiency criterion, however inadequate it may be considered.

4 CONCLUDING REMARKS

The above considerations have stressed the interactions existing between the decision-making process and evaluation techniques, such as CBA and MCA. When the features of such a process are taken into account, CBA may be considered still worth using but with a different perspective: no longer considered an ambitious tool for social choices but a useful informative system for public opinion.

Strangely enough, the existence of 'political constraints' provides further arguments to support the utilization of CBA because it makes evident the value judgements underlying the political decision-making process. At the same time, because information is improved, as Peacock (1979) points out, inadequate bureaucratic behaviour may be revealed. The analysis cannot modify such behaviour but different institutional relationships among those taking part in the decision-making process bear relevant consequences on its effectiveness as an evaluation tool.

Institutional relationships also affect the impact of MCA on the public decision-making process. Indeed these relationships influence the quantity and quality of information originated by the evaluation process and, as a consequence, the transparency of decision making will vary.

NOTES

1. Such a divergence has been considered one of the causes of the occurrence of the so-called 'collective failure', that is the incapability of public intervention to correct market imperfections (see, Wolf, 1979, 1983). On the grounds of these considerations, the scholars following this approach support the reduction of the size of the public sector. Some shortcomings of such an approach have been stressed by Bosanquet (1984).
2. As is well known, a principal–agent relationship exists when one party, the agent, agrees to act on behalf of another party, the principal. The challenge in such a relationship arises whenever, as is usually the case, the principal cannot perfectly and costlessly monitor the agent's action and information is not freely available. Moe (1984) suggests caution in applying straightforwardly the principal–agent paradigm to the public sector.
3. The most traditional 'checks and balances' are the existence of two Houses and the division of powers.
4. Analyses of such a concept from various standpoints are developed in Breton *et al.* (1990).
5. Actually not only intragovernmental but also intergovernmental competition does occur because local governments can apply for FIO funds; on intergovernmental competition, see the following subsection.
6. If financial constraints do not exist an overexpansion of public expenditure may occur as a consequence of such a perverse functioning of the political market (see Rizzo, 1985).
7. There exists a wide literature on the fiscal illusion issue, resulting from the pioneering contribution of Puviani (1903). Buchanan (1964) has extensively explored this issue; for a recent survey, see Oates (1988).

BIBLIOGRAPHY

Bosanquet, N. (1984), *La rivincita del mercato*, Bologna: Il Mulino.
Breton, A. (1987), 'Towards a Theory of Competitive Federalism', *European Journal of Political Economy*, 3, (1–2), pp. 263–329.
Breton, A., Galeotti, G., Salmon, P. and Wintrobe, R. (eds) (1990), *The Competitive State*, Dordrecht: Kluwer Academic Publishers.
Breton, A. and Wintrobe, R. (1982), *The Logic of Bureaucratic Conduct*, Cambridge: Cambridge University Press.
Buchanan, J. (1964), *Public Finance in Democratic Process*, Chapel Hill: North Carolina Press.
Campen, J.T. (1986), *Benefit, Cost and Beyond. The Political Economy of Benefit–Cost Analysis*, Cambridge, Mass.: Ballinger Publishing Company.
Dasgupta, P., Sen, A. and Marglin, S. (1972), *Guidelines for Project Evaluation*, Vienna: United Nations Industrial Development Organization.
Florio, M. (1990), 'Cost–Benefit Analysis and the Control of Public Expenditure: An Assessment of British Experience in the 1980s', *Journal of Public Policy*, (2), pp. 103–31.

Gramlich, E.M. (1981), *Benefit–Cost Analysis of Government Programs*, Englewood Cliffs: Prentice-Hall.

Haveman, R. (1980), 'Public Choice and Public Economics: the Case of Collective Failure in U.S. Water Quality Policy', in K.W. Roskamp (ed.), *Public Choice and Public Finance*, Paris: Cujas, pp. 137–54.

Margolis, J. (1980), 'The Public Investment Model and the Public Choice Process', in K.W. Roskamp (ed.), *Public Choice and Public Finance*, Paris: Cujas, pp. 113–26.

Mishan, E.J. (1982), 'The New Controversy about the Rationale of Economic Evaluation', *Journal of Economic Issues*, (1), pp. 29–47.

Moe, T. (1984), 'The New Economics of Organization', *American Journal of Political Science*, (4), pp. 739–77.

Mueller, D. (1987), 'The Growth of Government: A Public Choice Perspective', *IMF Staff Papers*, no. 34, pp. 115–49.

Muraro, G. (1990), *Central Appraisal and Financing of Local Projects: Physiology and Pathology*, paper presented at the 46th IIPF Congress, Bruxelles, 27–30 August.

Oates, W. (1988), 'On the Nature and Measurement of Fiscal Illusion: A Survey', in G. Brennan *et al.* (eds), *Taxation and Fiscal Federalism: Essays in Honour of Russell Mathews*, Canberra: Australian National University Press, pp. 65–82.

Peacock, A.T. (1973), 'Cost–Benefit Analysis and the Political Control of Public Investment', in J.N. Wolfe (ed.), *Cost Benefit and Cost Effectiveness Analysis*, London: George Allen & Unwin, pp. 17–29.

Peacock, A.T. (1979), 'Appraising Government Expenditure: A Simple Economic Analysis', in A.T. Peacock, *The Economic Analysis of Government and Related Themes*, Oxford: Martin Robertson, pp. 118–26.

Pennisi, G. and Peterlini, E.M. (1987), *Spesa publica e bisogno di inefficienza*, Bologna: Il Mulino.

Puviani, A. (1903), *Teoria dell'illusione finanziaria*, Palermo.

Randall, A. (1985), 'Benefit Cost Analysis of Environmental Program Alternatives: Economics, Politics, Philosophy and the Policy Process', *Ricerche Economiche*, pp. 483–90.

Rizzo, I. (1985), 'Regional Disparities and Decentralization as Determinants of Public Sector Expenditure Growth in Italy (1960–1981)', in F. Forte and A.T. Peacock (eds), *Public Expenditure and Government Growth*, Oxford: Blackwell, pp. 65–82.

Tresch, R.W. (1981), *Public Finance: a Normative Theory*, Plano: Business Publications.

Walsh, H.G. and Williams, A. (1971), *Current Issues in Cost–Benefit Analysis*, CAS Occasional Papers, no. 11, London: HMSO.

Wolf, C. (1979), 'A Theory of Non-Market Failure: Framework for Implementation Analysis', *Journal of Law and Economics*, **22**, pp. 1074–1139.

Wolf, C. (1983), '"Non–Market Failure" Revisited: the Anatomy and Physiology of Government Deficiencies', in H. Hanusch (ed.), *Anatomy of Government Deficiencies*, Berlin: Springer–Verlag, pp. 27–42.

Index

accidents, transport planning and, 86–8, 89
accounting rate of return, 9–10
activity profile, 55
aggregation methods, 73–4
aircraft industry, 20
Akehurst, R.L., 115
analysts
   bureaucratic role of, 151–3
   external consultants role of, 153–4
   public decision makers and, 148–51
annuity depreciation, 21–2
Ansoff, H.I., 7
appraisal *see* project appraisal
Arrow, K., 19
Ash, D., 4, 7
Audit Commission, 139

Banta, H.D., 123
Battiato, S.E., 37, 38
Beardwood, J., 99
Beesley, M.E., 83
behavioural models, 51
Bignell, V., 4, 22, 140
Bliss, C.J., 4
block grant finance, 135, 137, 141, 143–4
Bly, P.H., 92
Boeing 747, 5–6
Bowman, C., 4, 7
Braat, L.C., 44
Brealey, R., 4, 18, 20, 21
Breton, A., 162
Buchanan, J., 137
budget-maximizing, 141
Bulthuis, R., 116
bureaucracy, 151–3
   see also political factors
Buxton, M.J., 123

Cabasés, J.M., 113

Cairns, J. 122
Campen, J.T., 166
capital asset pricing model, 18
capital resource management, 3–7
Carr-Hill, R., 137
central government and local investment projects, 133–44
chain of transformations, 52
Chernick, H., 133, 141
Cleland, D.I., 4
coal industry, 20
Coburn, T.M., 83
cognitive process, 52
Cohen, D., 113
Community Impact Evaluation, 93, 102, 103
compensation principle, 27, 66–7, 69
competition, governmental, 162–5
concordance analysis, 53
Concorde, 4–7
conflicts of interest, 137–8
constrained maximization principle, 16
consumer surplus, 14–16
continuous evaluation methods, 46
corruption, 143
cost–benefit analysis (CBA), 65–7
   aggregation in, 73–4
   analysts' role in, 148–54
   compared with multicriteria methods, 154–6, 167–8
   distributional aspects of, 30–34, 68–9
   health care case study of, 106–23
   national planning and, 36–7
   objectives and constraints of, 26–7
   preparation work for, 74–6, 79
   public choice and, 37–8
   public decision-making process and, 146–51, 158–67
   social discount rate in, 34–5
   transport case study of, 83–103
   valuation of gains and losses in, 69–73

see also project appraisal
cost-effectiveness analysis, 108–9, 112
cost-utility analysis, 72, 109–10, 112, 114, 121
Cribb, A., 113
Culyer, A.J., 107, 114

Dasgupta, A.K., 89
Dasgupta, P., 159
Davies, L.M., 116, 122
Davy Corporation, 6
debt charges, 22–3
decentralization, 129–30, 143–4
   advantages of, 130–31
   forms of, 131–41
   negative effects of, 142–3
   spillovers from, 141–2
decision profile, 55–6
decision support systems, 59–60
decision trees, 21, 122
decision-making approach to CBA, 108, 117, 159
decision-making process, public, 146–51, 158–69
depreciation, 21–2
developing countries, 32, 117, 133
developmental effects of transport projects, 92–3
diagnostic technologies, 113–14
discount rate(s), 18, 34–5, 122
discounted cash flow, 8, 14, 23
distributional (equity) considerations, 15–16, 30–34, 68–9
   health care and, 121–2
   public investment and, 136–7
   transport planning and, 93–5
Dodgson, J.S., 92
Donaldson, C., 121
Drummond, M.F., 106, 109, 112, 113, 114, 116, 118, 119, 122

economic conditions, 19–20
economic policy, 138–40
efficiency, 66–7
   trade-off with equity of, 68–9
efficiency shadow prices, 33–4
electricity industry, 20
Elixhauser, A., 106
Elliott, J., 99
environmental issues, 44–5, 46, 59–60

transport planning and, 89–91
equity *see* distributional considerations
European Community, 130, 138
evaluation *see* project appraisal
Evans, R.G., 107
ex post monitoring, 21–3
expected utility, 20–21
expected value method, 53
external consultants, 153–4
externalities, 16, 28, 141–2
externalization of costs, 137–8

Feeny, D., 119
Finkler, S.A., 118
fiscal federalism, 136
fiscal illusion, 166
Fisher, Irving, 7
Flanagan, R., 4
Florio, M., 37, 160, 163
forecasting in transport planning, 88–9
formula funding, 137
Fortune, J., 4, 22, 140
Foster, C.D., 83
Fowkes, A.S., 85
Freksa, C., 52
French, S., 4, 21
Fuchs, V., 107
fuzzy set theory, 51–2, 63–4

Gafni, A., 119, 120
Generalized Consumer Surplus, 15
Giardina, E., 37
Gini Coefficient, 34
Ginzberg, M.J., 59
Glass, N.J., 121
goal programming methods, 54
goals achievement method, 53–4
Graham, J.D., 112
Gramlich, E.M., 165
Grossman, M., 107

Harberger, A.C., 33
Harman, R., 92
Haveman, R., 164, 166
Haycox, A., 113
health and health care, 20, 23, 106–7, 123
   assessment of costs and benefits in, 70, 71–2, 116–21, 122
   decentralization of investment in, 134–5, 139, 140–41

distributive issues in, 121–2
  forms of CBA used in, 107–12
  uses of CBA in, 112–16
health state valuations, 118–19
Heitger, L.E., 4
Helliwell, B., 112, 113
Henderson, J., 113
Henderson, P.D., 4
Hirshleifer, J., 7
Hochman, H.M., 136
Hoehn, J.P., 37
human capital, 108, 118, 121
Humber Bridge, 4, 6, 22, 140

Ibbs, Sir Robin, 129
ideal point models, 54
incentives, 17–18, 22–3, 129
income effects, 133–4
index of health, 72, 119
  see also Quality Adjusted Life Years
indirect effects, 28
inflation, 21
information, 49–51, 129, 137
  fuzzy set theory and, 51–2
integrated transport planning, 101
interest rates, 34–5
intergenerational issues, 35
intergovernmental competition, 164–5
internal rate of return, 11–13
intragovernmental competition, 162–4

Janssen, R., 56, 60
Johanesson, M., 121
Jones, T., 135
Jones-Lee, M.W., 87, 112
Jönsson, B., 121

Kanafani, A., 88
Kettle, P., 93
Kharbanda, O.P., 4
Kind, P., 119
King, W.R., 4
Knill-Jones, R.P., 114
Kreidel, 115
Kristiansen, I.S., 113

land use effects of transport projects, 92–3
Leitch, Sir George, 90
Leitch framework, 90–91, 93

Levine, M.N., 114
Lichfield, N., 93, 115
Lind, R., 19
local authorities, 22–3, 101
  local investment projects, 130–44, 164–5
Loomes, G., 119, 120
Lorenz Curves, 34
Lowson, K.V., 115
Luce, B.R., 106
Luce, R.D., 51
Ludbrook, A., 109

M1 motorway, 83
McHugh, G., 4
McKenzie, L., 119, 120
Mackie, P.J., 92, 101
McKinnon, A.C., 92
macroeconomic policy, 138–40
managerial incentives, 17–18, 22–3
Marglin, S., 159
Margolis, J., 166
Markandya, A., 89
market price, 28, 69
Marks, P., 85
Marsh, R., 139
Marshall, A., 14
Matulich, S., 4
May, A.D., 101
Maynard, A.K., 114
Mayston, D.J., 15, 17–18, 21, 22, 23, 130, 137, 39, 140, 141, 144
measurement theory, 49
Mehrez, A., 119, 120
membership functions, 63–4
merit goods, 136
Mills, A., 117
min-max models, 54
Mishan, E.J., 29, 34, 146–7, 159
Monte Carlo simulations, 21
Morgenstern, O., 118
Mueller, D., 161
Mugarra, I., 113
multiple criteria evaluation methods, 44, 47, 48–9
  compared with CBA, 154–6
  public decision-making and, 167–8
  transport planning and, 56–9, 101–2, 103
  typology of, 53–6

multiple internal rates of return, 12
Muraro, G., 28, 142, 165
mutually exclusive projects, 12–13
Myers, S., 4, 18, 20, 21

Nash, C.A., 31, 85, 90, 93, 97
national planning, CBA and, 36–7
Nelson, R.H., 146
net present value, 7–9, 12, 17, 18
net social benefit, 14–16
Neuburger, H., 122
Nijkamp, P., 44, 46, 56
Nimrod project, 4
Niskanen, W., 141
non-profit performance indicators, 17
Norman, G., 4
Nuti, F., 28

organization of health care, CBA analysis of, 115

Pareto criteria, 26, 66–7, 68–9, 106, 159
Parsonage, M., 122
Paulley, N.J., 92
pay-back period, 11
Peacock, A.T., 166, 168
Pearce, D.W., 31, 89, 90, 93
penalty models, 54
Pennisi, G., 163
performance-related pay, 18
Peterlini, E.M., 163
Petretto, A., 31
Planning Balance Sheet, 93, 102, 103
planning process, 36–7, 43, 45–8
political factors, 6–7, 29–30, 31, 33, 65–6, 72–3, 74
  decentralization of investment and, 140–41, 142, 143
  public decision-making and, 147–8, 159–67
  transport planning and, 94
Porter, M., 7
portfolio investments, 19
poverty index, 34
Preston, J., 97
prevention of disease, 113
price(s)
  market, 28, 69
  shadow, 28–9, 32–4, 35, 160

principal/agent relationships, 161
private sector
  ex post monitoring in, 21–2
  investment appraisal in, 7–13, 16–17, 23
  risk and uncertainty in, 18–19
privatization, 3
progressive movement, 146–8
project appraisal (evaluation), 3, 23–4, 60–61
  capital resource management, 3–7
  cost–benefit analysis and, 26–38, 74–7
  decision support systems for, 59–60
  ex post monitoring in, 21–3
  information precision in, 49–51
  fuzzy set theory and, 51–2
  managerial incentives and, 17–18, 22–3
  multiple criteria methods of, 48–9
    example of application of, 56–9
    typology of, 53–6
  planning process and, 43, 45–8
  policy making and, 43–5
  private sector, 7–13
  public decision-making process and, 146–51
  public sector, 14–17
  risk and uncertainty in, 18–21, 49–51
  transport case study of, 83–103
project finance decentralization, 129–44
Prowle, M., 135
public choice, CBA and, 37–8
Public Choice Theory, 150, 161
public sector
  cost–benefit analysis in, 26–38
  decision-making process in, 146–51, 158–69
  ex post monitoring in, 22–3
  investment appraisal in, 14–17, 23
  investment decentralization in, 129–44
  managerial incentives in, 17–18, 22–3
  privatization of, 3
  project failure in, 3–7
  risk and uncertainty in, 19–21, 23
public transport, 95–9

qualitative information, 49–50

fuzzy set theory and, 51–2
Quality Adjusted Life Years (QALYs), 22, 109–10, 114, 119–22
quality of service targets, 17–18, 22

Raiffa, H., 51
railway projects, 83, 92, 95–9, 100
Randall, A., 37, 160, 166
regime analysis, 56
resource allocation theory, 26
return on equity, 10
return on investment, 10
Reynolds, D.J., 83
risk and uncertainty, 18–21, 23, 49–51, 122
road schemes *see* transport
Roberts, F.S., 49
Rodgers, J.D., 136
Rosser–Kind index, 119
Russell, I.T., 114

safety issues, 86–8, 89
Sanderson, I., 83
Schmid, A.A., 37, 77
Schweitzer, S.O., 117
Sen, A., 159
sensitivity analysis, 21, 122
Separation Theorem, 7
settings for care, CBA assessment of, 114
shadow prices, 28–9, 32–4, 35, 160
shipbuilding industry, 20
Silberberg, E., 15
Simon, D., 92
Simon, H.A., 51
Sinclair C5 car, 6
Smith, P., 137
social discount rate, 34–5
social shadow prices, 33–4
specific risks, 19
spillovers (externalities), 16, 28, 141–2
Squire, L., 32, 33
Stallworthy, E.A., 4
Stanley, J.K., 93
Stason, W.B., 119
steel industry, 19, 20
stewardship concept, 22
Stiglitz, J.E., 31
stochastic uncertainty, 50–51
Stohr, E.A., 59

straight-line depreciation, 21
strategic considerations in transport planning, 99–101
subsidiarity, 130
substitution effects, 134
Sugden, R., 107
supermarkets, 19
systemic risk, 18–21

taxation, 9–10, 133
telecommunications industry, 20
Thompson, M.S., 121
Thomson, J.L.G., 113
Tiebout model, 132, 136
time, transport planning and, 85–6, 89
time preference, 34–5
time value of money, 7–8, 21
Torrance, G.W., 119, 121
trade-off analysis, 53
transport and transport planning, 20, 46, 70–71, 83–4, 103
  appraisal methods for 84–8
  alternative, 101–2
  context of, 99–101
  comparison of modes of, 95–9
  environmental effects of, 89–91
  forecasting methods for, 88–9
  income distribution and, 93–5
  land use and development effects of, 92–3
  multiple criteria evaluation methods in, 56–9, 101–2, 103
  strategic considerations in, 99–101
treatment, CBA assessment of, 114
Tresch, R.W., 159
Tullock, G., 137

unanimity rules, 138
uncertainty and risk, 18–21, 23, 49–51, 122
utility models, 54
utility theory, 51, 118–19

valuation, assumptions in, 69–73, 116–21
value for money assessment, 21–2
Van Der Tak, H.G., 32, 33
Van Lierop, W.F.J., 44
Vaupel, J.W., 112
Victoria Line, 83

Von Neumann, J., 118

Wager, R., 117
Walsh, H.G., 160
Warner, K.E., 106
water industry, 20
Webster, F.V., 92
Weinstein, M.C., 119
Weisbrod, B.A., 108

welfare economics, 26, 66, 68, 106, 160
Whitbread, M., 93
Williams, A., 22, 32, 107, 119, 122, 160
Wilson, R., 4
Wintrobe, R., 162
World Bank, 33
Wright, K.G., 114

Zadeh, L.A., 51, 63